The Last Rebbe
of Bialystok

To Elizabeth

Enjoy

Neil M. Levy

The Last Rebbe
of Bialystok

Neil M. Levy

RED OAK TREE PRESS

Berkeley ∼ California

For information contact:
Red Oak Tree Press
P.O. Box 7326
Berkeley, CA 94707
neil.levy@comcast.net

ISBN 978-0-615-22827-3
Library of Congress Control Number
2008942124

Printed in the United States of America

Book design: Steven Zahavi Schwartz
Text set in Cochin/Ruach display

CONTENTS

In loving memory of my father Abraham Levy who came from Bialystok and to my mother Rose Levy who did not.

And to the memory of Rabbi George Vida and Rebbitsin Emmie Vida with whom I learned Torah and learned to love learning Torah.

Thanks to the wonderful people who make up the Torah study group at Congregation Beth El, Berkeley, California.

And thanks to the generous support of the Bratton/Wruble Writer-in-Residence-Program.

And deepest gratitude for the support of my wife Jane Levy.

INTRODUCTION

Some say the last Rebbe of Bialystok died as a young man in the Treblinka death camp. Others claim that no such person ever existed, that the man and woman who would have been his parents were killed at Treblinka — before they even met.

There is evidence, however, that the man who should have become the Bialystoker Rebbe was taken to Treblinka and survived, but could not take his place as Rebbe since his community had been destroyed.

> A survivor of the death camps met the Rebbe and asked how there could be historians who doubt the Holocaust occurred. The Rebbe replied, "Don't judge them too harshly. I was at Treblinka and I cannot believe what occurred."

This tale, while attesting to the existence of a folk legend about a final Bialystoker Rebbe, may not prove he actually existed. Rabbis of long ago taught that all Jews, past, present and future, heard the law at Mount Sinai. Perhaps then, the legend that the Rebbe survived Treblinka should only be understood in the sense that all Jews — past, present and future — lived, died and yet survived Treblinka.

What is clear is that legends about the life and teachings of the Rebbe persist, often in incongruous times and places. For example, some claim to have heard the Rebbe's voice on the radio, never distinctly, but through static on distant sounding stations.

I, myself, have never heard the Rebbe's voice. I am a secular scholar by trade, studying and teaching the often arcane rules of insurance law. I am without formal training in the ways of Torah. Yet as my life became entwined with the legends and sayings of the Rebbe, I read and reread the Torah, and commentaries about it, to understand better the teachings attributed to him.

I did not originally seek out the Rebbe, though at times I feel as if he allowed me to stumble across his path. I travel extensively in my profession and when I began to hear legends and teachings of the Rebbe, I recorded them in the same lap-top computer I use in my professional life. These stories surfaced not only in Prague and New York and Tel Aviv, but in more unlikely locales, such as the Cook Islands in the South Pacific.

As I became more involved with the material I collected, I noted that legends about the Rebbe, and sayings attributed to him, often took on the tone of the place where I found them. For example, sayings I came across in Poland had the flavor of East European Jewry, even though Poland now has virtually no living Jewish community.

At first, I did little more than to categorize and collate material. Later, I tried to do more methodical research, but without much success. The Rebbe has no entry in the Encyclopedia Judaica, nor in the Library of Congress catalogue. My searches on the internet were equally fruitless. Even today, after I've accrued a great deal of material, I would not guess whether a Last Rebbe of Bialystok actually existed. How I gathered my material is not the point. I have become weary of trying to determine his existence and am no longer certain it even matters. The legends about the Rebbe, and the sayings attributed to him, are repositories for certain teachings, whether the Rebbe is viewed as a creature of flesh and blood or merely as a projection of a disrupted culture. I think of myself as a scribe who had the fortune to come across these teachings and legends.

At times I feared that if I exposed the Rebbe to the light of day, he might somehow vanish. But I also feel duty bound to take that risk in order to attempt to spread his knowledge. His teachings were from ancient sources, but seemed relevant today.

MIDRASH

In Hebrew, the word "midrash" (plural "midrashim") means "to search out [meaning]." The word has a specific connotation within Torah study. Torah contains statements that read literally are incomplete, or unclear, or contradictory, or troublesome, or even (to some), abhorrent. The most common type of midrash provides explanations for such "difficult" passages. But the Rebbe also recognized another type of midrash. He taught:

> Some midrashim simplify the complex. Others add layers of depth to the seemingly simple. Though starting at opposite points, the two types meet at a middle ground.

To traditional Jews, when Moses received the written law at Mount Sinai, he also received additional oral teachings, including all midrashim. Some traditionalists insist that the term "midrash" should only be used to refer to explanations compiled before the Thirteenth Century. The Rebbe's view is different.

> One day, the Rebbe told a midrash to his congregation that no one had heard before. He was asked how could there be a new midrash if all Torah, written and oral, had been given at Mount Sinai? The Rebbe answered:
> From where do you think my midrash comes?

The Rebbe taught that every thought, written or spoken, that explains Torah is a midrash. Every act of kindness explains Torah's teaching.

APPROACHING THIS BOOK

Jewish tradition divides the Torah, the Five Books of Moses, into 54 portions, (in Hebrew: singular — parashah; plural — parashiyot). Most weeks, virtually every synagogue in the world will read the same parashah, according to a calendar devised centuries ago. I have arranged this book parashah-by-parashah.[1] In this book, each right hand page contains a midrash from the Rebbe about particular concepts in that week's parashah. This page should be read before the facing left hand page.

As I compiled material about the Rebbe's life, I noted that it was not just the Rebbe's midrashim that were tied to a particular parashah; often, legends about him also appeared tied, albeit more loosely, to specific portions. It is as if the Rebbe treated life itself as an interpretation of Torah, based on the principle that the more difficult the text, the greater the need for explanation. Therefore, opposite each midrash, I have placed a legend that also clarifies that week's portion.

Many of these legends contain parables. The Rebbe taught that legends and parables reach levels underlying understanding. To explain their importance, he would tell:

THE PARABLE PARABLE

A teacher wished to explain the nature of a sphere to a young child. Because only square blocks were available in the classroom, the teacher was unable to help the student grasp the concept.

After class, the child played with a ball in the schoolyard.

On the bottom of each page, I refer to sources, and sometimes offer my own comments about the material. I hope that my notes clarify more than they confuse. I assure the reader that I have tried to remain absolutely faithful to ambiguities in the Rebbe's thoughts. I do not believe those ambiguities to be errors in transmission, but rather to be evidence that the Rebbe's thoughts often were not linear. Passages may yield multiple meanings upon multiple readings.

---

[1] By custom, the name of each week's Torah portion is the first significant word in it that has not been used to name a prior portion. For example, the first portion is "Bereshit," which means "In the beginning" or "At the beginning."

It need not be your goal to read this short book in a sitting or two. It is commentary on Torah. As an aid to study, it can best be understood when read in conjunction with reading the week's parashah. The Rebbe himself was reputed to have said:

> Midrash explains Torah.
> Since midrash answers text,
> text explains midrash.

Many readers, (like myself) may not have sufficient skill to read Torah in Hebrew. This is unfortunate since any translation into English is, by necessity, tainted by the translator's psyche. However, a legend about the Rebbe teaches that at least one advantage can come from reading the Bible in English, rather than in Hebrew:

> A Jew who did not read Hebrew, but studied Torah in English, once said to the Rebbe,
> "How wonderful that you can read the Bible in Hebrew. I only read it in translation."
> The Rebbe replied:
> "To speak to us, the Holy One had to translate the message into human thought, human language. When you read the Bible in English, you read a translation of a translation. I sometimes forget that Torah in Hebrew is itself a translation."[2]

---

[2]In setting out English translations of Bible verses, I have primarily relied upon the Jewish Publication Society's 1917 translation as it appears in the Hertz, *Chumash*, Soncino Press (2d Edition, 1960); the Jewish Publication Society's 1962 translation as set out in Plaut, *The Torah*, Union of American Hebrew Congregations (1981); and the more recent translation of *The Five Books of Moses* by Everett Fox, Schocken Books (1995). Occasionally, I meld translations.

בראשית

Bereshit

Genesis

BERESHIT legend

After studying with the Rebbe for the first time, a student asked him the purpose of Torah study. The Rebbe answered:

A messenger[1] visited a factory and noticed a beautifully carved and decorated box. He asked a worker what was in the box, and the worker explained that the box housed a tool whose very purpose was to carve and decorate the box.

ૐ ૐ ૐ

A disciple asked the Rebbe whether he believed that the Torah came from God. The Rebbe responded:

It is better to pretend the Five Books come from the Holy One, than to pretend they do not.
"Why?" asked the disciple?
"It's cold in winter," answered the Rebbe.

---

[1]In Hebrew, as in ancient Greek, the word for "angel" stems from a word literally meaning "messenger."

BERESHIT

Genesis 1:1–6:8

*T*he Torah that the Holy One gave to Moishe[2] was not the first Torah. Adam was not the first Adam, and Eve was not the first Eve. This Creation was not the first, nor need it be the last. All is subject to change, allowing those who study Torah to participate in *tikkun olom* — the repairing of the universe.

ﺷ ﺷ ﺷ

God said, Let there be light. And there was light.[3]
How could the Holy One create
    light and dark,
    day and night,
three days before creating
    the sun
    and the moon
    and the stars?[4]

The sculptor sees the statue
    — later strikes the stone.[5]

---

[2]Many midrashim that I collected in Europe use the Yiddish name "Moishe" for "Moses."

[3]Genesis 1:3.

[4]Genesis 1:16.

[5]The Rebbe taught, "Since Torah contains poetry, midrash must contain poetry."

NOACH legend

Aﬂfter an evening of study, his student[6] told the Rebbe, that he was troubled that midrashim were in conflict even over so simple a line in Torah as, *Noach was a righteous, wholehearted man in his generation....*[7] The student knew that some midrashim argue that Noach was so upright that even in a corrupt era he was able to remain righteous. While others conclude that Noach was only righteous in comparison to his corrupt generation.

The student said, "Rebbe, it seems as if there is a different midrash for every Jew who ever lived." The Rebbe answered:

> More than that! For every Jew who ever lived, there is a separate midrash for every verse in Torah — perhaps for every word — or even for every letter. And each is constantly changing.

---

[6]Many legends tell of the Rebbe teaching a student or disciple. Students in these legends often take on individualized personalities though are never identified by name.

[7]Genesis 6:9.

NOACH[8]

Genesis 6:9–11:32

O f every living thing, of all flesh, two of every sort bring into the ark....[9]

Because Noach knew the legend about his ancestors Adam and Eve in the Garden, he asked whether HaShem[10] wanted even two snakes to be brought aboard. And the Holy One answered:

> Had it not been for the snake, Adam and Eve would still be in the Garden, without children. Noach, you owe your life to the snake. Yes, take two of *every kind of creeping thing of the ground*....[11]

அ அ அ

> After the flood,
>   even after the rainbow,
> no matter how thirsty he became,
>   Noach could not pray for rain.

---

[8]When Hebrew is transliterated into the English alphabet, *ch* is pronounced as is *ch* in the composer's name Bach. Noach is the Biblical name for Noah.

[9]Genesis 6:19.

[10]Traditional Jews do not vocalize certain names of God, except in prayer or while publicly reading the Torah. "HaShem," which means "the Name," is often used instead. Rabbinic literature contains many names for God, such as "The Eternal" or "The Rock." Some Jewish mystics were said to be able to produce miracles by manipulating the Holy Names. The Rebbe of Bialystok said, "The names of the Holy One are too numerous to count because the manifestations of the Holy One are too numerous to count."

[11]Genesis 6:20. It seems clear that the Rebbe rejects the doctrine of "original sin."

LECH LECHA legend

A neighbor visited the Rebbe for advice. "Rebbe," he said, "my son plans to move from our small town, to the capital many miles away." The man knew he would miss his son a great deal, and he feared the son might abandon their ways, or even Judaism itself once he left the town.

The Rebbe told the father that he understood his anguish and asked whether the man had educated his son in the ways of Judaism. The man said that he had and the Rebbe responded:

> Having your son these years has been a blessing. No guarantees come with children. Certainly you will miss your son. But remember, it is the way of the son to challenge the way of the father. Abram left his father Terah when he was told to do so by the Blessed Holy One.
>
> Let us pray that your son, like Abram, is on a mission for the Holy One.[12]

---

[12] I have never met anyone who claimed to be a child of the Rebbe. In fact, I never came across any legend about the Rebbe having a child or a wife, except for the following nonsensical "Noodle Pudding" poem that some congregations attribute to the Rebbe and sing in jest on Purim, the holiday of mirth:

> I may be too humble
> to admit that I'm humble
> but my wife makes a great *lukshen kugle*.

LECH LECHA

Genesis 12:1–17:27

*W*hen the Most Holy said to Abram, *Go forth from your land, from your kindred, from your father's house*....[13] Abram asked, "Where am I to go?" And the Blessed One answered, *To the land I will show you.*[14]

Abram asked, "Why should I leave my land, my kindred, my father's house when I don't even know my destination?" And HaShem told him *Go forth...I will bless you.*[15]

So Abram left, and set out with his nephew Lot, not knowing that he and Lot would be blessed with so many sheep and with so many oxen that they would have to live apart since *the land was not able to support them.*[16]

Abram learned that being blessed is not always a blessing.

---

[13]Genesis 12:1.
[14]Same.
[15]Genesis 12:2.
[16]Genesis 13:6.

VAYYERA   legend

The Rabbi was visiting a small town where he was not known. As Shabbat approached, he found a *shul* (synagogue) where he could pray. Though there were many pious men in the congregation, all noticed how the Rebbe prayed, with *kavanah* (intensity), and with his eyes always focused on the page.

After services, a member of the congregation approached the Rebbe and said, "You pray with the *kavanah* of our father Abraham. I see how well you know your prayers. You must have them memorized. Why must you concentrate so intently on the pages?"

The Rebbe answered:

> I can recite the prayers without reading them. I am not looking at the page in order to recite the words. The *Mashiach* (the Messiah — the savior) may arrive at any moment. But before the Mashiach arrives, all the letters in all our prayer books must raise up, so that those letters can help raise the dead.
>
> If I pray with enough intensity while reading the prayers perhaps I can help lift the letters from their pages and speed the coming of the Mashiach."

VAYYERA

Genesis 18:1–22:20

*I*f there are fifty innocents within the city [Sodom] will you really sweep it away?[17]

჈ ჈ ჈

Now there was a famine in the land and Abram went down to Egypt.[18]

Some say that Abram left Haran to avoid a spiritual famine, just as he later left Canaan and journeyed to Egypt to avoid a physical famine. Others hold that Abram did not need to leave Haran, or even Ur, to spread belief in Yud Hey Vov Hey.[19] He could have done that from anywhere.

In truth, Abram had to leave Haran so that he could reach Sodom in time to pray that it be spared. That his prayer was not answered always grieved him.

---

[17]Genesis 18:24.

[18]Genesis 12:10.

[19]These four Hebrew letters spell God's most holy ritual name. In ancient times, only the High Priest was allowed to pronounce that name. He would pronounce it, indistinctly, once a year, on the Day of Atonement, while standing in the Holy Place.

CHAYYE SARAH legend

*O*n a cold, sunny day in winter, a member of the Rebbe's congregation walked on the north side of the town's main street. The sun had been out all morning and had melted the ice from the night before. On the south side of the street, where buildings shaded the walkway, ice still lingered. As the man walked, he noticed an alley that led from the south side of the street to the town's park. The park was sunlit, with walkways and benches dried by the sun.

As he wondered whether he should continue to walk in the sun, or cross through the shade to reach the park, the congregant saw the Rebbe approaching and posed his dilemma. The Rebbe responded, "To complete a journey, one must begin it." The congregant, still frightened, said "The other sidewalk is slippery. I might fall." And the Rebbe answered, "Yes, you might. What an ideal opporunity to learn about ice!"

CHAYYE SARAH

Genesis 23:1–25:18

*T*erah, Abraham's father, left Ur intending to go to Canaan. But he stopped in Haran,[20] never reaching his destination. When Torah states that the iniquities of the fathers will be visited on the third and the fourth generation,[21] it means that failure to follow a path to its conclusion requires others to complete the journey.

Eliezer and then Jacob returned to Haran so that Rebecca,[22] Rachel and Leah could complete Terah's outward journey for him. When the Kingdom of Judah was conquered, Terah's descendants were taken to Babylon, near the ancient city of Ur, to complete the outward journey yet again.

Had Terah foreseen all this, he still would have stopped in Haran. Having foreseen it all, he could have laughed, knowing that he was a prophet.

---

[20]Genesis 11:31.
[21]See Exodus 20:5.
[22]Genesis 24:58 *And she* [Rebecca] said: *"I will go."*

TOLEDOT legend

A student asked the Rebbe, "What must I do when my understanding of Torah differs from views of our ancient sages?" The Rebbe told him the eyeglass parable.

> An old man noticed that his sight had deteriorated and that his eyeglasses no longer corrected his vision sufficiently to allow him to read. He went to an eye doctor who provided him with a new pair.
>
> All went well until the day the old man misplaced his new glasses at home. Because his vision was so weak, he was unable to see well enough to find where he had left the new pair. But he remembered where he had left the old. Although the old glasses were not strong enough to allow him to read, they were adequate to allow him to find the newer pair.

The Rebbe continued:

> Be like Isaac. Isaac first found and cleared the wells dug by his father Abraham. Only afterward did he open his own wells.[23] There will be times when your views differ from those of our sages. At such times you must remember the words of Torah: *Do not turn your face to ghosts*...[24]

---

[23]Genesis 26:18.
[24]Leviticus 19:31.

TOLEDOT

Genesis 25:19–28:9

hen famine came to Canaan, Isaac pleaded that the Lord let him go to Egypt, as his father Abraham had been permitted to do during a previous famine. But the Holy One refused to allow Isaac to go.[25] Though Isaac's wealth soon increased a hundredfold,[26] late at night, Isaac often felt trapped within the land he had been promised and wondered what the trip to Egypt would have been like.

ۻ ۻ ۻ

Esau was a man who knew the hunt, a man of the field, but Jacob was a quiet man, staying among the tents.[27]

When Isaac was old, he pretended to believe Jacob when Jacob pretended to be Esau. Esau was the elder brother, but he loved to hunt. Because Isaac knew the feeling of being trapped, he did not wish to trap Esau into the sedentary life of being the clan's spiritual leader.

Despite Jacob's motivation, Esau felt betrayed and Jacob filled with guilt.

---

[25]Genesis 26:2.

[26]Genesis 26:12.

[27]Genesis 25:27. In rabbinic tradition, Jacob the tent dweller studied and taught the ways of God.

VAYYETZE legend

One evening, a workman came to study with the Rebbe. They had not studied together for some time and the Rebbe asked him how he had been. The worker answered, "Like Jacob in Haran, my days are filled with labor. There are days that I work so hard, I come home too tired to study Torah, to read the blessed words."

The Rebbe replied:

On those days, just read the spaces between the words.

The workman asked, "Is there Torah in the spaces between the words?" and the Rebbe answered:

Meaning in the spaces? I suppose so. But I meant there is Torah in a hard day's work.

VAYYETZE

Genesis 28:10–32:3

*T*he Holy One told Jacob, *Your seed will be like the dust of the earth.*[28] Jacob also knew that the Blessed One also had told Abraham and Isaac that their descendants would be as numerous as the *stars in the sky.*[29] Jacob understood these promises meant that his descendants would be numerous.

But Jacob also knew that these promises contained warnings; at times, Jacob's descendants would be tread upon by the powerful and kicked about as the wind blows grains of dust. And as clouds can blot out the stars, so too, at times, his children and his children's children would be blotted from view.

Since Jacob heard these silent warnings, after twenty years of hard labor for Laban in the East,[30] he still had hesitations about returning to Canaan.

---

[28]Genesis 28:14.
[29]Genesis 15:5, 26:4.
[30]Genesis 31:38.

VAYYISHLACH legend

A mourner said prayers at his mother's grave. As the Rebbe passed, the mourner asked him, "Will my mother hear my prayers?" The Rebbe answered:

> The dead are dead, I cannot ask them. When I was a child, I heard my grandfather, may he rest in peace, say that the dead don't care how the living treat them; they only care how mourners treat each other.

The mourner asked, "Then why do I light a *yahrzeit* candle on the anniversary of my mother's death each year?

And the Rebbe answered:

> Though we never can understand the "world-to-come,"[31] while a *yahrzeit* candle burns, it is as if the loved one is in the room.

"There are times I am fearful of death and wish to know what comes after." And the Rebbe replied:

> Who knows the form of formlessness or the reason why?[32]

---

[31] Although the Torah makes no explicit reference to an afterlife, the concept permeates later rabbinic Judaism.

[32] When I visited the memorial at the Treblinka death camp, I heard this legend from a fellow visitor. It was at Treblinka that the Nazis murdered the Jewish community of Bialystok.

VAYYISHLACH

Genesis 32:4–36:43

*O*n his way to Aram, when Jacob dreamt of the angels and the ladder, he heard HaShem tell him *I am with you. I will watch over you wherever you go.*[33] Jacob misunderstood and thought that the Holy One would travel with him, which is why he answered, *Yud Hey Vov Hey was in this place and I did not know it.*[34]

Twenty years later, as Jacob returned, he heard HaShem say *I will be with you.*[35] Jacob again misunderstood, thinking that the Holy One, like Laban's idols, could come and go and be carried about.

Jacob had to wrestle with the messenger[36] before he could re-enter Canaan. Only after HaShem entered Jacob's body, causing pain, injuring his leg, renaming him Israel, did Jacob understand that the Eternal One need not move in order to remain with him.

Because he became Israel, he could accept reunion with Esau. But because he had been Jacob, the reconciliation was incomplete. He would see Esau again only at the burial of their father Isaac.[37]

---

[33]Genesis 28:15.
[34]Genesis 28:16.
[35]Genesis 31:3.
[36]Genesis 32:25–32.
[37]Genesis 35:29.

VAYYESHEV legend

THE MARBLE BUILDING PARABLE[38]

"Rebbe, as I approached a marble building, a messenger tapped my shoulder, pointed to a bench at the building's corner and told me to sit and guard the building each night, from sunset to sunrise. He said there was only one door to the building and pointed. But I could not see the door because the building was long and its entrance was recessed behind a colonnade.

"I have done as he asked. Night after night I guard the building from my bench. No one comes, no one goes. Some nights as dawn approaches, I think I see a faint light spilling out, as if the door has opened a crack. But still, until this morning, I sat.

"This morning at dawn, I saw the light again and could sit no longer. I left my bench, walked through the colonnade and saw that indeed there was a door, opened a crack. I peeked in and saw a golden room, a room larger than the building itself. I ran from the building, away from the room, knowing I must be gone before sunrise.

"Rebbe, I am troubled. After all this time, even after this morning, I do not know whether my task is to keep people from going into the building or from leaving. Tell me.

The Rebbe appeared to go into a trance. At last, shortly before sunset, he spoke to the man:

> You mistook what the messenger said, or at least what he meant. Your task is to safeguard the building. To do this, you must prepare yourself to enter the building, to enter the room itself.

"Rebbe, I have not even begun this, my task."

> Yes. There is time, if you hurry. Pay attention to the entrance as dawn approaches. If you see a bright light or even one that is faint, enter my friend, enter. The Mashiach, the Messiah, may be counting on your presence.

---

[38]Some legends about the Rebbe, such as this one, have too dreamlike a quality to be taken literally. It seems likely that this legend emanated from a dream that someone brought to the Rebbe to be interpreted.

VAYYESHEV

Genesis 37:1–40:23

After Joseph's brothers sold him into slavery, they dipped his coat, the coat of many colors, into blood and brought it to Jacob, to deceive him. Though Jacob said that *an evil beast must have devoured* Joseph,[39] he had not been misled. He meant that hatred among brothers devours, as if it were an evil beast.

Jacob grieved deeply. He grieved for the loss of Joseph. He grieved for the souls of Joseph's brothers. And he grieved for opportunities he had missed with his own brother, Esau.

ﻼ ﻼ ﻼ

When Joseph asked the Pharaoh's cupbearer and baker *are not interpretations from God?*[40] he did not actually believe that God was the sole source of the interpretations. At the time, all Joseph really knew was that he had been sold into slavery because of his brothers' anger over his childhood dreams.[41] Joseph was frightened to take personal responsibility for the interpretation of his fellow prisoner's dreams.

---

[39] Genesis 37:33.
[40] Genesis 40:8.
[41] Genesis 38.

MIKKETZ legend

*T*he Rebbe had a disciple with a brilliant mind who reminded him of the young Joseph: brilliant, but arrogant or at least self-absorbed. On Shabbat Mikketz,[42] after services, but before his customary Shabbat nap, the Rebbe studied the week's parashah with this student. The Rebbe told the student,

> Joseph fed his brothers, the very brothers who had sold him into slavery, not because he loved them, nor even because they were his brothers, but so that the story could continue. It is for this reason alone that it is written, *Joseph knew his brothers, but they knew him not*.[43]

The student answered, "I don't understand this midrash. What use is a midrash beyond comprehension?" The Rebbe answered,

> Whenever I hear one it changes my life.

---

[42]Traditionally, Jews dated events in their lives by the name of the parashah of the week.
[43]Genesis 42:8.

MIKKETZ

Genesis 41:1–44:17

The *yetzer hara* (the evil inclination) of Joseph's brothers sold Joseph into slavery in Egypt. Joseph's *yetzer hara* caused him to inflict anguish on his brothers when they first arrived in Egypt, falsely accusing them of being spies[44] and making them fear they would also be accused of theft.[45]

Because of the effect of Joseph's tricks on them, his brothers were able to repent. Joseph then realized that all his dreams and all his interpretations of dreams — those of his childhood, those in the dungeon, and those of the fat and lean years — truly were prophecy. Since the Holy One brings forth dreams, Joseph could forgive his brothers after he learned to treat their deeds as if those too had been dreams. He could then say to his brothers, *It was not you that sent me here, but God*.[46] Since Joseph had falsely accused them of acts they had not committed, the brothers were able to accept Joseph's forgiveness for those acts they had committed.

Thus, Joseph came to realize that even the *yetzer hara* can help accomplish the goals of the Heavenly One.

---

[44]Genesis 42:9.
[45]Genesis 42:25.
[46]Genesis 45:8.

VAYYIGGASH legend

A young man from a Jewish family came to the Rebbe and said, "Rebbe, my parents were born Jews, but they are not observant. I am angry that they gave me no connection to things Jewish. I now wish to learn." The Rebbe asked him whether his parents were alive, and he answered yes.

The Rebbe thought and said:

> It is good that you seek what you seek. Like our father Jacob, you may need to meet the Holy One face-to-face to reach your peace.

The student said how difficult that would be for him and the Rebbe responded:

> Meeting the Holy One may be difficult for you. But before you can know genuine peace, you must reach out to your family and pursue reconciliation. If you do not, your peace, like that of Jacob's with Esau, may be only illusory. But be clear, achieving reconciliation with your family may be more difficult than meeting the Holy One.

VAYYIGGASH

Genesis 44:18–47:27

After twenty-two years, when Jacob again saw Joseph, they had much to ask each other. Joseph wanted to know why his father had sent him out to meet his half-brothers, the brothers who Jacob knew hated Joseph. Jacob wanted to know why his favorite son Joseph, even after becoming the Pharaoh's viceroy, had not sent back word that he was still alive.

There are some who say that Joseph immediately forgave his father when they met. Others say he did not do so until Jacob reminded him that they both were children of Yud Hey Vov Hey, the God of Abraham and Isaac.

But in truth, we do not know all of what was said between the two. There are things so private, such as a father and a son reconciling, that Torah will not disclose exactly what occurred.[47]

---

[47] Frequently midrashim fill gaps in the Torah narrative.

VAYYECHI legend

*T*he Rebbe once visited an old man who was near to death. The man told the Rebbe that he was not prepared to die. The Rebbe asked him whether he had enjoyed his life, and the man answered that, like Jacob, he had known much pain and family strife.

The Rebbe answered, "That does not matter now. Who is ever ready to awake from a dream?"

৵ ৵ ৵

The Rebbe once visited an old man who was near to death. The man told the Rebbe that he was not prepared to die. The Rebbe asked him whether he had enjoyed his life and the man answered that he had a wonderful family, good friends and sufficient money to be comfortable.

The Rebbe answered, "That does not matter now. Who is ever ready to awake from a dream?"

VAYYECHI

Genesis 47:28–50:26

*B*ury me with my ancestors in the cave that is in the field of Ephron
the Hittite in the cave that is in the field of Machpelah....[48]

Out of respect, Jacob speaks of joining his ancestors. But he
dreams of lying next to Leah whom he had buried in the cave. By
making his sons, the sons of both Rachel and Leah, agree to bury
him in Machpelah, Jacob assures that they will not fight over his
resting place. In death, Jacob repairs harm he committed by favor-
ing one child over another, one wife over another.

Rachel sleeps alone by the highway, weeping for all the children of Israel.[49] But she grieves most deeply for Dina, Leah's
only daughter.[50]

---

[48]Genesis 49:29–30.
[49]Jeremiah 31:15.
[50]It was the rape of Dina that led her brothers to destroy Shechem. Genesis 34.

שמות

Shemot

Exodus

SHEMOT legend

*T*he Rebbe sat in a coffee shop[1] with a student who pointed out a waiter and told the Rebbe, "Harry. All day long he runs back and forth. He works from eight in the morning till eight at night, like a slave in Egypt." The Rebbe asked, "does he provide for his family?" and the student answered, "He makes a living."

The Rebbe saw another man who was seated at a table talking, joking and having coffee with friends. "Tell me about that one," the Rebbe asked, "do those with him always seem so happy?" The student answered, "Yes, but Max never seems to do any work."

The Rebbe responded:

> It is permissible to tell jokes on Shabbat, but not to work. There is room for both Max and Harry in the world-to-come. Harry will laugh while eating a lunch cheerfully served by Max.

---

[1]Stories about the Rebbe that I first heard in America, such as the above, often have a more "modern" setting or tone than those I collected in Eastern Europe.

SHEMOT

Exodus 1:1–6:1

Moses saw the slaves,
    the slaves who toiled but multiplied,
    and sought the power of his God.

Moses saw the bush,
    the bush that burned but did not burn,
    and knew the power of his God.

And God heard the question,
    the question Moses did not ask,
    and gave Torah in answer.

VA-AYRA legend

am the Lord, I will free you from the burdens of the Egyptians and deliver you from their bondage.[2]

The Rebbe spent a Passover away from home. The president of the synagogue he had been attending invited him to celebrate the holiday with him and his family.

The president lived in a large, well-furnished home. After the pre-dinner service, an extremely lavish Seder dinner was served. During dinner all began to discuss issues raised by the Hagaddah, the book that tells the story of the Exodus.

The Rebbe was sitting next to the daughter of his hosts, who asked him. "Rebbe, was the Exodus God's greatest miracle?" The Rebbe answered:

> The Exodus was a great miracle. But the Holy One heard the children of Israel groaning and remembered his covenant.[3] God had to free the Israelites.
>
> The greatest of all miracles is that entire days go by when we need no miracle.

---

[2]Exodus 6:6.
[3]Exodus 6:5.

VA-AYRA

Exodus 6:2–9:35

A mram took himself Yocheved his aunt as a wife, and she bore him Aaron and Moses.[4]

El Shaddai, (God Almighty) gave Moses no task more difficult than this: Moses was asked to teach Torah. Torah commands to honor one's father and mother and Torah commands that a man may not marry his father's sister.[5] Yet Moses knew that his father Amram had married Yocheved and that Yocheved was Amram's father's sister.

It is said in the world-to-come, all Israel shall assemble to hear the angels sing praises to Amram and Yocheved. Only after the births of their children, Miriam, Aaron and Moses could marriages between nephews and aunts be prohibited and Torah be delivered to the people of Israel.

---

[4]Exodus 6:20.
[5]Leviticus 18:12.

BO legend

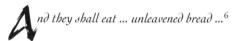

nd they shall eat ... unleavened bread ...[6]

As the Rebbe packed for a journey, a disciple noticed that he wrapped a tiny piece of matzah and placed it in his suitcase. He asked the Rebbe why he had done this and the Rebbe answered:

> The matzah I packed is part of the afikomen from this year's Passover seder. A Persian Jew once told me that the power of the afikomen, the matzah which we eat to end the meal, is so great that to carry a small uneaten part of it on a journey, assures a safe return.

"Rebbe," the student asked, "Do you believe this *bubbe-meiseh?*"[7]

> I could tell you "Yes."
> I could tell you "No."
> I could tell you "It couldn't hurt."
> But in truth, who am I to argue with a Persian Jew.

---

[6]Exodus 12:8.
[7]Literally grandmother's tale. In Yiddish usage: a fanciful story.

BO

Exodus 10:1–13:16

Because Moses was slow of speech,[8] he feared his task. He knew he would lead his people to freedom because the Holy One had promised that the Israelites would be delivered from Egypt.[9]

But, Moses knew the legend of his ancestor Abraham pleading with God to spare the people of Sodom. Moses knew that unless he spoke with power and conviction, Pharaoh would not let the Israelites leave Egypt soon enough to avoid the ten plagues.

After the death of the Pharaoh's firstborn son,[10] the brother of the very woman who had taken Moses from the river, Moses felt failure, disgrace. When he asked why firstborn infants, even firstborn animals, were slaughtered, the Holy One answered:

> *Ehyeh asher ehyeh*.[11]
> I am that I am.
> I will be what I will be:
> > Yud Hey Vov Hey.

---

[8]Exodus 4:10. Some say Moses was slow of speech because he stuttered.
[9]Exodus 3:8.
[10]Exodus 12:29.
[11]Exodus 3:14.

BESHALLACH legend

*O*n hearing a joke he enjoyed, the Rebbe would recite the following blessing

Blessed are you Lord our God, Ruler of the universe who commands us to bring forth mirth.

Each joke, he taught, hastened the coming of the Messiah.

ぷ ぷ ぷ

When the Rebbe first learned English, he sensed the language's potential and asked, "Who took the fun out of fundamentalism?"

ぷ ぷ ぷ

The Rebbe once told a gathering of American Jews:

When Moishe learned that English speaking Jews called the Torah, the Five Books of Moses, he asked, "Who is Moses?"

When he was told that Moses was his name in ancient Greek, he asked, "Who were the Greeks?"

Moses picked up a chumash,[12] looked inside and said, "Five books? There's some very good work in the other three?"

ぷ ぷ ぷ

When asked why Hebrew is read from right to left, he replied,

Because that's the way it's written.

---

[12]A printed book containing the books of the Torah.

BESHALLACH
Exodus 13:17–17:16

As the pursuing army of the Pharaoh grew near, the children of Israel became frightened and cried out to Moses: *Is it because there are no graves in Egypt that you have taken us out to die in the wilderness?*[13]

Moses thought of telling the people to meditate on the names of the Holy One,[14] but instead he laughed and answered,

"Joke at your anguish and you will survive."

---

[13]Exodus 14:11.

[14]There is an alternative midrash also attributed to the Rebbe.

    The Israelites asked Moses to tell them all of the names of the Holy One so they could use them to protect themselves from the Egyptians. Moses answered:

    To learn the names,
    follow the paths
    of the Holy One.
    Deeds create morality.
    Morality is measured in deeds.

YITRO legend

A student studying parashah Yitro with the Rebbe commented on the lack of clarity of the narrative. She said it was difficult to follow the time sequence of the Covenant and the revelation of the Torah. She said to the Rebbe, "I cannot follow the story." The Rebbe responded:

> If clarity were the goal, we would have received a different Torah, one easier to understand.

The student returned in several days and told the Rebbe that she had studied the portion again, along with the parallel account in Deuteronomy,[15] yet still she could not understand the narrative. The Rebbe answered:

> Study Torah near the edge:
> near the edge of the river,
> near the edge of the sea,
> near the edge of the city.
> Don't study Torah in peace,
> Study Torah near the edge of peace.

---

[15]Deuteronomy, chapter 5.

YITRO

Exodus 18:1–20:23

When creating the universe, God did not knew whether the Israelites would accept the Covenant.

On the mountain, Moses said to the Eternal, "I don't know if the people will accept the terms of your Covenant. They already complain about being in the desert. Since you are almighty, force the people to accept."

The Holy One answered,

> Without acceptance from the heart,
> there can be no revelation.

Because they accepted the Covenant, God called the Israelites *my special treasure*,[16] and made them a *kingdom of priests*.[17]

---

[16]Exodus 19:5.

[17]Exodus 19:6. The Rebbe's midrash seems to respond to a traditional midrash that the Israelites accepted the Covenant only because God lifted the mountain above their heads and threatened to drop it on them if they did not.

MISHPATIM legend

*O*ne night, an old woman came to see the Rebbe and told him that at home she had carelessly eaten a piece of meat with utensils she used for dairy products. The woman was an observant Jew and kept utensils for milk products separate from those for meat. The Rebbe could see how upset she was over this mistake. He said to her:

> The rabbis of the Great Assembly said, "Make a fence around the Torah."[18] Generations of rabbis multiplied rules forbidding Jews from mixing dairy products and meat. But, all these rules were meant to help Jews follow the simple Biblical command, *Do not boil a kid in its mother's milk.*[19]

The Rebbe continued:

> The purpose of the fence is to help avoid situations where, even inadvertently, you are in danger of breaking a commandment. But if the fence is too high, it can prevent you from embracing Torah. If the fence is also too thick, it can prevent you from seeing the Torah, or even knowing it exists.

The woman then asked, "Is there nothing I need to do?" And the Rebbe answered:

> Do not allow yourself to be saddened by guilt. Bury the utensil for three days so that, once again, it becomes fit for use for dairy.

When the woman asked "why," the Rebbe answered:

> Because it is our custom.

---

[18]Pirke Avot 1.1. *Pirke Avot, Ethics of the Fathers*, is a book of the Mishnah.
[19]Exodus 23:19.

MISHPATIM

Exodus 21:1–24:18

*T*orah states that *"Moses was on the mountain for forty days and forty nights."*[20] Yes, the Israelites waited forty days and forty nights for Moses to return, but on the mountain itself,

> there were no days.
> there were no nights.
> there was no time.

The children of Israel thought that Moses had delayed in order to spend more time with the Holy One. But, of course, if there is no time, there can be no delay.

When the Israelites asked Moses whether the Holy One had explained all Torah to him on the mountain, he answered that God had spoken, but had used no words.

---

[20]Exodus 24:18.

TERUMAH legend

*T*he Rebbe noticed his student becoming restless as they studied parashah Terumah with its intricate instructions for building the Tabernacle.[21] The student said:

> As I read this week's parashah, it became difficult for me
> to assume that a God, ruling this universe, would choose
> to communicate with humans through the medium of five
> written books and then devote so many of those words to
> describe one dwelling.

The Rebbe replied:

> at times, to be a Jew is to live a fiction.

---

[21]The Dwelling — the *Mishkan* — the Tabernacle — was the movable structure whose construction is detailed in Exodus. It housed the ark of the
Covenant which in turn held the tablets of the ten commandments. In the
desert, Moses would go to the Dwelling to receive revelation.

TERUMAH

Exodus 25:1–27:19

Even before God gave the Torah, Moses begged that the Israelites be allowed to build a sanctuary. God replied, *I am everywhere. What need have the Israelites to confine me?*

Moses answered:

> My Holy One, it is your needs that concern us. When people do not have a home near their loved ones, they can feel abandoned, alone. Since we are created in your image, I thought that perhaps you need a home near us, your loved ones.

God laughed and said, *Let them build me a Holy Shrine, that I may dwell among them.*[22]

---

[22]Exodus 25:8.

TETZAVEH legend

On the high priest's tunic, *You are to make on its skirts* [woven] *pomegranates....*[23]

A man who could vocalize the Hebrew alphabet, but could not grasp the language's meaning, once asked the Rebbe what should he do when the Torah was being read in the synagogue. Should he follow the sounds of the text in Hebrew or should he read its meaning in an English translation?

The Rebbe answered,

> The shape of the pomegranate is beautiful.
> Sweetness surrounds its seeds.

---

[23]Exodus 28:33.

TETZAVEH

Exodus 27:20–30:10

God told Moses *speak to all that are wise-hearted, whom I have filled with the spirit of wisdom...*[24] and tell them to make Aaron's priestly garments. But when Moses spoke to the Israelites, they thought only of all the work required.

The Israelites, even the wise-hearted, were not happy. Moses had also told them that only Aaron and his descendants could be priests.[25] The Israelites sent a delegation of leaders, one from each tribe, to Moses. They said, "Since all Israel is a kingdom of priests,[26] why should only your brother Aaron, and his descendants, be permitted to officiate in the Tabernacle?"[27]

And Moses answered, "Because that is what God commanded. Isn't it enough for you that the Shechinah[28] will live in your midst?"

And the leaders answered back, "Unless you are planning to do all the weaving and sewing by yourself, you must at least satisfy us that Aaron will act as our delegate to the Holy One, and will not meet with God merely for his own personal benefit."

Moses thought this request fair and that it presented no difficulties. He told the delegates that the Blessed Holy One had already met this demand as it is said that Aaron must wear a robe with *a golden bell and a* [woven] *pomegranate, a golden bell and a pomegranate... so that sound may be heard whenever he comes into the Holy Shrine before the presence of Yud Hey Vov Hey and whenever he goes out, so that he does not die.*[29]

Thus, all the children of Israel would be able to hear and keep track of Aaron as he approached the Holy of Holies.

---

[24]Exodus 28:3.

[25]Exodus 28:1.

[26]See Exodus 19:6.

[27]Korach used this argument to foment the Great Rebellion against Moses. See Numbers, Chapter 16.

[28]The Living Presence. In mystical Jewish traditions it is usually associated with the feminine aspects of God.

[29]Exodus 28:34–35.

KI TISSA legend

The Last Rebbe of Bialystok awoke to hear the music of the universe playing silently in a minor key. Chaos, he knew, lurked beneath seeming order. Yet, he suspected that he would become confused in a universe he understood.

The Rebbe said that he could not comprehend the reason Moses broke the sacred tablets. But the Rebbe kept searching for an answer. He would say:

> A non sequitur in Torah is merely a linear connection not
> yet understood.

KI TISSA

Exodus 30:11–34:35

As he neared the camp in which the Israelites had made the Golden Calf, *Moses' anger flared up and he threw the tablets from his hands and smashed them beneath the mountain.*[30]

And God asked Moses:
Why did you smash the tablets?
    Why, in anger, did you smash
    the tablets of the law I gave for you to keep?
You smashed them in anger,
You smashed them against the very mountain where we meet.

And Moses answered:
I am created in your image.
The image of the God who would,
    in anger, have consumed the very people
    he did love.[31]
I consumed only stone.

Thus, it is written: *Yud Hey Vov Hey spoke to Moses as a man speaks to his friend.*[32]

---

[30]Exodus 32:19.
[31]See Exodus 32:10.
[32]Exodus 33:11.

VAYYAKHEL legend

A student said to the Rebbe, "At times the words of the Torah seem as precious to me as the gold used to cover the Holy Ark. I hate to admit it, but sometimes I am reluctant to share my thoughts with my fellow students." The Rebbe praised him for recognizing that this was a problem and then told him the *Vault Parable*:

> A miser purchased a vault from a traveling salesman and placed all his most valuable items inside. Since the key to the vault was now his most precious possession of all, he locked it inside as well.

The Rebbe then continued and told the student the *Wine Bottle Parable*:

> A large wine bottle, filled to the top, stood next to a smaller, empty one of the same shape. When the larger bottle was tipped, wine flowed into the smaller vessel, but the larger one did not appear to empty.
>
> With wine in it, the smaller bottle appeared to be in the image of the larger. When it, in turn, was used to fill still other bottles, although the level of wine in it went down, the remaining wine appeared to become more rich in color.

VAYYAKHEL

Exodus 35:1–38:20

The Holy One had expected Aaron not only to be the High Priest, but also to supervise construction of the Tabernacle. To test him, God had kept Moses on the mountain until the Israelites had given Aaron their gold.

That Aaron had cast a graven image,[33] an image of a neighbor's god, did not anger God. The Holy One was angry that the Golden Calf was of such shoddy workmanship, knowing that if Aaron were careless even in sin, he could not be trusted to build with care the sacred Tabernacle. God instead chose Bezalel, who was not a priest, but whom the Holy One *filled with the spirit of God, in wisdom, in understanding, and in knowledge, and in all manner of workmanship.*[34]

This is why in David's Kingdom, though the Levites washed the feet of the priests, the people loved the artist and the poet and the builder.

---

[33]Exodus 32:4.
[34]Exodus 35:31.

PEKUDY legend

*T*he Rebbe thought it important to teach his students the rabbinic tradition that Torah does not always present its story in chronological order. He often taught using time play.

A short poem attributed to the Rebbe reads:

> Think Torah in the present tense.
> Speak Torah in the present tense.
> Live Torah in the present tense.
>> It happened long ago.

PEKUDY

Exodus 38:21–40:38

For the cloud of Yud Hey Vov Hey was upon the tabernacle by day and there was fire by night, before all the House of Israel, throughout all their journeys.[35]

By the end of Shemot, Exodus, the Book of Going Forth from Egypt, the Holy One forgives the Israelites for their Golden Calf and continues to provide them manna. The Shechinah again dwells in their midst, leading them to their promised land.

If Torah ended here, we would complete the reading of the Torah cycle by returning to Bereshit, for surely we would be back in the Garden of Eden. Since this time Adam and Eve would choose to avoid eating from the Tree of the Knowledge of Good and Evil, Torah could not be given and there would be no second cycle, nor third.

But, of course, there are Five Books of Moses and the Israelites had thirty-eight more years to spend in the desert.

---

[35]Exodus 40:38, the final verse in the book of Exodus.

ויקרא

Vayyikra

Leviticus

VAYYIKRA legend

The Lord called to Moses and spoke to him from the Tent of Meeting....[1]

When the Last Rebbe of Bialystok first reached the atoll of Aitutaki[2] in the South Pacific and met its High Priest, as was the custom, they shared fermented coconut sap. As the evening neared its close, the Priest thought about the Rebbe's life story and said, "You have travelled much, you have learned much. I have never left this atoll."

And the Rebbe answered:

> Maybe you are the wise one. When my people were in the desert, going from slavery to their homeland, they constructed a holy ark. The Shechinah, the Living Presence, would reside in the midst of their camp, right above the ark. When the Presence rested, the tribes would rest. When the Presence rose, my people would break camp and follow.
>
> Perhaps my friend, for you and your people, the Shechinah dwells on this very atoll, allowing you to remain here in peace. I must confess, like my ancestors in the desert, there are times when I can only try to reach the Presence before it moves on yet again.

---

[1]Leviticus 1:1.

[2]Though Aitutaki — an atoll in the distant Cook Islands — is an unlikely locale to find a rabbi, a fair number of legends I collected concern the relationship between the Rebbe and the atoll's traditional High Priest. These legends may be apocryphal or have occurred in more mundane locations. When I visited Aitutaki, I found no Jews living there. I asked numerous islanders whether they knew of the Last Rebbe of Bialystok and they only could tell me that foreigners had lived on their atoll for periods of time.

VAYYIKRA

Leviticus 1:1–5:26

*T*he parashah that begins Vayyikra, Leviticus, the Book of the Law of the Priests, ends by describing laws governing theft.[3]

If there has been theft, before there can be forgiveness, there must be justice. The lawgiver must speak, the judge must reach moral judgment and the thief must make restitution.[4] Only then may a priest perform the sacrifice for forgiveness.

Though Aaron and his sons alone could perform the ritual of sacrifice for atonement, Vayyikra therefore must begin *And Yud Hey Vov Hey called to* Moses....[5]

---

[3]Leviticus 5:23–26.
[4]The person committing the theft must *restore that which he took by robbery....* Leviticus 5:23.
[5]Leviticus 1:1.

TZAV legend

An old Jewish woman on Aitutaki approached the Rebbe and told him that at times when she would read Torah on Shabbat, she would have seemingly profound, dreamlike insights. Since she was observant, she could not write them down until after Shabbat ended. But by that time, she often had forgotten the thoughts. She asked the Rebbe whether her thoughts therefore amounted to nothing.

The Rebbe answered:

> Wasted? Hardly. The Holy One uses forgotten thoughts
> to create the world-to-come.

TZAV

Leviticus 6:1–8:36

This is the law of the burnt offering[5A]

*T*he Eternal One filled the days of the priests with the drudgery of detail in order to keep them from turning towards mischief. Each priest had to learn, understand and be able to carry out each and every detail found in parashah Tzav concerning offerings.

Each of the other children of Israel had to memorize only one verse of Tzav, so that collectively they could determine whether their priests were properly fulfilling the commandments.

Therefore, to this day, a child of Israel who studies just one rule about sacrifice on Shabbat Tzav can rest for the remainder of the day.

[5A]Leviticus 6:2.

SHEMINI legend

These you are not to eat...the pig....[6]

As the High Priest of Aitutaki became closer to the Last Rebbe of Bialystok, he asked him one day, "Rebbe, why do your people not partake of the meat of the pig?"

The Rebbe asked in turn, "Doesn't day follow night, and night follow day?" Confused, the Priest said, "Why does day follow night and night follow day? Rebbe, I don't follow the relevance of your question."

The Rebbe paused, smiled and answered, "Exactly."

---

[6]Leviticus 11:7.

SHEMINI

Leviticus 9:1–11:47

*M*oses read the laws concerning sin offerings to his nephews, Aaron's sons, Nadav and Avihu, the day before they were to take office as priests.

That night, Nadav said to Avihu,

"As priests, we will eat of the sin offerings."
And Avihu agreed.
"Then the more that people sin, the more we get to eat."
And Avihu agreed.
"Then I do not wish to be a priest," said Nadav.
And Avihu agreed.

In the morning, Nadav and Avihu lit a strange fire at the altar, knowing that they would become the sacrifice. The Holy One took their lives, but saw into their hearts. As they died they were not alone, God was with them, for it is written, *and they died before the Presence of Yud Hey Vov Hey.*[7]

---

[7]Leviticus 10:2.

TAZRIA legend

One day, the High Priest came to the Rebbe and said, "One of my people has a skin rash which is not getting better. I've heard you say that your holy book explains how to cure rashes. Rebbe, can you cure this man."

Priest, I wish I could, but I really can't. You are right that our Book tells what to do with certain rashes. Unfortunately, the cure doesn't work.

"Rebbe why do you study a book that gives you solutions that do not work?"

I can't tell you why our Book contains a remedy that does not work. I only know that the Book our Holy One gave to us is meant to be read with one's mind as well as one's heart. If our Torah, or ancient comments by our sages about our Torah, do not appear to be correct, we can't make believe they do. We must search for a new interpretation.

TAZRIA

Leviticus 12:1–13:59

... *he shall cry out Tamei! Tamei!*[8]

A person with *tzaraat*, (a skin disease which some say means leprosy) must not only be told by the priest that he is *tamei* (which some say means unclean), but must cry out, "*Tamei! Tamei!*" By shouting this truth, the one with tzaraat transforms the accusation into an act of self-acceptance, accepting the physical condition but rejecting moral blame.[9]

Torah states that one with *tzaraat* must remain alone for at least seven days, outside the camp.[10] By leaving the community, the one with *tzaraat* supports the community. Though no person is allowed to be with him, by shouting out "*Tamei! Tamei!*" he opens himself to the company of the Shechinah.

Had Nadav and Avihu not lit the strange fire at the Tabernacle, they could have explained this to the children of Israel.

---

[8]Leviticus 13:45.
[9]The Rebbe is rejecting rabbinical commentary that *tzaraat* is punishment for slander.
[10]Leviticus 13:46.

METZORA legend

he one to be cleansed shall...bathe in water; then he shall be pure.[11]

On Friday afternoon, as was his custom when on the atoll of Atutaki, the Last Rebbe of Bialystok went to a tidal pool with his good friend, the island's High Priest. The High Priest sensed that something was bothering his friend and inquired.

The Rebbe told the Priest that he wished he could have one clear, unmistakable sign of the existence of the Blessed Holy One to whom he had dedicated his life. The High Priest arose and said to his friend, "It is best that you be alone."

The Rebbe floated in the pool, letting the warm ocean water relax his muscles. While floating, he noticed the half moon, already high in the sky well before sunset. He saw the monumental shapes of tropical clouds and watched an egret soar. He stood up and looked at the outer reef, waves crashing as usual and he watched the tide flow in as it did twice each day.

When the Rebbe left the water, the High Priest went to his friend and asked, "What did you see?" The Rebbe answered, "I saw no sign."

The Priest persisted. "I asked what you saw, not what you did not see." And the Rebbe told him of the moon and the clouds and the egret and the waves and the tide. The High Priest continued, "Weren't these all signs from your Holy One?" And the Rebbe responded, "I see them everyday."

The Priest replied, "If today, you had seen any of these for the first time, you would have considered it a sign, a miracle. How much more so that your Holy One lets you see them everyday."

The Rebbe thought about his friend's words and knew that the signs were there if only he knew how to look.

---

[11]Leviticus 14:8.

METZORA

Leviticus 14:1–15:33

Yud Hey Vov Hey spoke to Moses saying[12]*....Then the priest is to dip his right finger in some of the oil that is on his left palm and is to sprinkle some of the oil with his finger, seven times, before the presence of Yud Hey Vov Hey....[and so on].*[13]

When reaching the verse about dipping, the Blessed Holy One realized that Moses no longer was listening very closely. The Eternal said, "Moses, purification of the body is important. Listen." And Moses answered, "I can no longer tell what is holiness and what is magic."

And God answered, "If you barely pay attention to the rules of purification of the body, then you will not listen to the rules for purification of a house. Call your brother, your brother Aaron, the High Priest — he will listen."

This is why Torah, before giving instruction on purification of houses in Canaan, says, *Yud Hey Vov Hey spoke to Moses and to Aaron, saying....*[14]

---

[12]Leviticus 14:1.

[13]Leviticus 14:16.

[14]Leviticus 14:33. Comparing this midrash with the one for Vayyikra, it seems clear the Rebbe thought of Aaron and Moses not only as brothers, but also as partners in leading the Israelites.

ACHAREY MOT legend

*E*ven on Aitutaki, during Elul, the month that precedes Rosh Hashanah and Yom Kippur, the Rebbe would remember a conversation he had many years ago with Solomon, the prayer leader of a small shul on New York's Lower East Side.

Solomon saw and recognized the Rebbe and said to him:

> I am told you are a sage. Last year my firstborn son fell ill on Rosh Hashanah and died of the illness on Yom Kippur day. When a messenger told me of the death, I could no longer lead prayers. In the days that followed, I became angry at myself for this failure of faith. My anger continues today — but now it is directed towards God. Why should I confess to the God who took my son, my first born son?

The Rebbe answered:

> There were years that I too could not confess on Yom Kippur. I looked at the world, the pain, the hunger, the cruelty and I asked, how serious are my sins in comparison? Why should I confess to a God that allowed Cain to kill Abel, a God who would have killed the Israelites, if Moses did not intercede?
>
> And then one Kol Nidre[15], instead of confessing to God, I demanded that God confess to me: confess for the pain, confess for the hunger, confess for the cruelty.
>
> As the day of the fast lengthened, as Ne'ilah, the closing prayer, approached, again and again, I demanded a response. When the congregation recited the last Vidui,[16] I finally heard a voice, a voice saying:

> > There is balance in asymmetry.
> > There is harmony in discord.
> > Chaos underlies order, but order underlies chaos.

Solomon asked the Rebbe whether hearing that voice had brought him peace and the Rebbe answered, "Once again, I can beg forgiveness."

And Solomon asked, "So you accepted God's confession?"

And the Rebbe answered:

God's confession? You think the Holy One confessed to me? No, my friend, I still seek an explanation.

❧ ❧ ❧ ❧ ❧ ❧

ACHAREY MOT

Leviticus 16:1–18:30

Aaron shall cast lots on the two goats, one lot for Yud Hey Vov Hey and one lot for Azazel.[17]

Torah states that on Yom Kippur, the Day of Atonement, one goat is to be sacrificed to Yud Hey Vov Hey and the other is to be sent to Azazel. But today, no one knows who or where or what is Azazel.

It is said that on the Day of Judgment, the meaning of Azazel will be revealed because it is only by first knowing Azazel that a soul can begin to know Yud Hey Vov Hey.

---

[15] Jewish holidays begin and end at sunset. The sacred Kol Nidre prayer begins the evening service that starts Yom Kippur.

[16] a confessional prayer

[17] Leviticus 16:8.

KEDOSHIM legend

*L*ate in the afternoon on the atoll of Aitutaki, the Rebbe saw many of the men, including the High Priest, frantically launching their small boats into the ocean, even though the waves were quite high and dangerous.

Several hours later, the boats returned, everyone seeming quite joyous. The Rebbe went down to the launching area and asked the High Priest what had gone on. The Priest told the Rebbe that one of the fishing boats had not returned to shore by 4:00 p.m. The Priest continued that whenever that happened, all the other fishermen would return to the ocean to try to find the missing boat before dark. They had done so today and had found the man on his disabled boat and brought him and his boat back to safety.

The Rebbe commented on how courageous it was for the men to go out on a day as rough as today. The High Priest responded, "Here on this island, Rebbe, we have an expression: *Love your neighbor as yourself.* Going back out today was just an example of this belief." The Rebbe responded, "My people have the same saying.[18] Some of my people even think that they alone among the peoples follow the rule." The High Priest answered, "Yes. Some of my people feel the same."

---

[18]Leviticus 19:18.

KEDOSHIM

Leviticus 19:1–20:27

*T*orah says *sanctify yourself*,[19] and in the next verse says, *I, Yud Hey Vov Hey, am the one who sanctifies you*. How can it be that the Holy One sanctifies, yet one can sanctify oneself? A parable explains:

> If a man takes a journey, he may think he accomplishes it alone. But, of course, he could not complete the journey unless provided with time and only the Eternal One creates time.

But what if the distance of the journey is too great to complete?

> Then the rules must be reinterpreted as it is written that God's commandments *are not too hard for you nor too far off*.[20] If a modern interpretation conflicts with an ancient one, the modern is to be preferred if it could not have been appreciated or accepted by our ancestors. Ancient interpretations existed to allow Torah to survive until the time those explanations could be revised.

---

[19]Leviticus 20:7.
[20]Deuteronomy 30:11.

EMOR legend

*t*he New Year shall be *proclaimed with the blast of horns*....[21]

As the High Priest of Aitutaki passed his island's tiny synagogue, he saw the Last Rebbe of Bialystok looking despondent.
He asked what was the matter and the Rebbe answered:

> There are days when I feel the complete indifference of
> the universe. On such days I continue to pray. There are
> other days when I think the universe is darker than that.
> Today is such a day. I have said my afternoon prayers, but
> without fervor.

The High Priest said to the Rebbe, "Come, my friend, the sun
is low, the waves are glassy." The Rebbe counted to be certain that
there still was a minyan[22] for the evening prayers and answered:

> Thank you Priest. Today I join you in the water. You sing
> your prayers to the ocean and I will whisper mine.

That night the Rebbe realized that a conch shell can sound like
a shofar.[23]

---

[21]Leviticus 23:24. Note that the holiday on the first day of the seventh
month, now celebrated as the Jewish New Year, is simply called a
"memorial" and a rest day in the Torah. See also Numbers 29:1.

[22]Ten Jews, the minimum number required in order to recite certain prayers.

[23]A ram's horn, cut so that it can sound a blast. It is used to awaken the spirit
on the Jewish New Year.

EMOR

Leviticus 21:1–24:28

*I*f we did not have the narrative (*aggadah*) about the blasphemer,[24] we would think that the rule is always *And he that blasphemes ... if he also pronounces the name Yud Hey Vov Hey, shall be put to death*.[25] But quite the opposite is true.

The Torah narrative tells us that the children of Israel did as the Blessed Holy One commanded.[26] All those who heard the blasphemer's profanity leaned *their hands on his head*.[27] Since anyone who tried to stone the blasphemer might by mistake hit one of these righteous accusers, the community threw their stones as required, but made certain they landed far from the blasphemer. It is only in this sense that Torah can state, *Moses spoke to the children of Israel. And they took the blasphemer outside the camp, and pelted him with stones*.[28] The children of Israel exercised intelligence and realized that stoning the blasphemer to death was prohibited since that might compound the blasphemy by injuring the righteous.

Of course, there is no problem today. Since no one now knows how to pronounce the Most Holy's most holy name, no one can be punished for saying it.[29]

---

[24]Leviticus 24:10–16, 23.

[25]Leviticus 24:16.

[26]Leviticus 24:23.

[27]Leviticus 24:14.

[28]Leviticus 24:23.

[29]After the Rebbe told this midrash, a congregant came to him and said, "Rebbe, your midrash explains a very difficult passage. But do you believe it is the true meaning of the story?"

The Rebbe answered, "I hope it is the meaning the Holy One intended."

BEHAR legend[30]

A student of the Rebbe, quite obviously shaken, asked, "How can the same parashah which says *Proclaim liberty throughout the land*,[31] also allow Israelites to own foreign slaves.[32] The Rebbe told him that it was not only permissible, but also mandatory for a Jew to feel that way. The Rebbe continued:

> One who hears verses allowing slavery without feeling revulsion and shame, has not read Torah. The Messiah cannot arrive until Israel chooses justice. Torah allows slavery only so that the children of Israel can reject it. You may not merely ignore these verses, you must confront them.

It is said that when verses allowing slavery were read in the synagogue, the Rebbe would shout to drown out the words, as if the name of Hamen were being read.[33]

---

[30]This legend, like last week's midrash, uses a broad principle of Biblical justice to reinterpret a seemingly harsh narrow provision.

[31]Leviticus 25:10.

[32]... *you may keep them as an inheritance.* Leviticus 25:46.

[33]In the Book of Esther, Hamen is an enemy of the Jewish people. The victory of the Jews of Persia over Hamen is celebrated on the holiday of Purim. A custom among Jews is that when reading the Book of Esther, children shout and use noise makers to drown out every mention of Hamen's name in the text.

BEHAR

Leviticus 25:1–26:2

*B*ut in the seventh year, there shall be a Shabbat of solemn rest for the land, a Shabbat of Yud Hey Vov Hey.[34]

Why must Torah tell us that the Shabbat year is *a Shabbat unto Yud Hey Vov Hey*? To remind us, *The earth is the Lord's and the fullness thereof.*[35]

Torah contains three types of Shabbat: one that comes every seventh day when work is prohibited; one that comes every seventh year during which year one cannot sow one's fields or prune one's vineyard; and, the Jubilee year[36] which comes after the seventh, seventh year, when land is returned to those who had lost it to creditors. All three teach the same principle: to avoid greed, to avoid being possessed by possessions and to avoid a sense of entitlement.

Torah tells us that plants which grow on their own during the seventh year can be eaten. But they do not belong only to the landowner. They must be shared with servants and sojourners as well.[37] The righteous would have deduced these rules merely from the concept of the weekly Shabbat, but they appreciate the rules being made explicit.

---

[34]Leviticus 25:4. From an early period, Rabbinic law held that Jews need only practice the Shabbat year and the Jubilee year in the Land of Israel.
[35]Psalms 24:1.
[36]Leviticus 25:8–55.
[37]See Leviticus 25:6.

BECHUKOTAI legend

During the celebration of the new moon, the High Priest of Aitutaki passed his island's small synagogue and heard the congregation singing the *Shechechianu*. He enjoyed the melody and after the service asked the Rebbe its meaning. The Rebbe translated the blessing:

> Blessed are you, Lord our God, Ruler of the Universe who has kept us in life, and preserved us, and enabled us to reach this season.

The Rebbe explained that the prayer is said when one reaches a happy or significant event, such as a holiday or a personal anniversary.

The Priest asked the Rebbe whether on Aitutaki it would be appropriate to recite a *Shechechianu* on the day the turtles return to lay their eggs. And the Rebbe answered, "Yes."

Or on the day each month when the mullet begin to run? And the Rebbe answered, "Yes."

Or the day that mangos first ripen? Or when a child falls and gets up uninjured? Or the rains start? Or stop? Or the evening of a particularly beautiful sunset?

And the Rebbe answered, "Yes. Yes. Yes. Yes. Yes."

And the High Priest said, "Rebbe, I do not understand this *Shechechianu*. Surely you must say this prayer every minute of every day and have no time left for doing anything else.

BECHUKOTAI

Leviticus 26:3–27:34.

*I*f you walk by my laws and keep my commandments....[38]

But if you do not hearken to me, by not observing all *these commandments*....[39]

When Torah states that Jews who fulfill the mitzvot will be blessed,[40] it means those who fulfill *every* mitzvah will be blessed. When Torah threatens a curse for not fulfilling the mitzvot, it carefully reserves that curse for those who do not observe *any* commandment. Torah contains 613 mitzvot. Anyone who fulfills every one will be blessed and anyone who fails to fulfill a single mitzvah will be cursed.

But from the time of Moses until this day, there has not been a single Jew who has fulfilled every commandment, nor a Jew who has failed to fulfill at least one. Therefore, no one's fate has been ordained.

[38]Leviticus 26:3.
[39]Leviticus 26:14.
[40]Leviticus 26:3–12.

במדבר

Bemidbar

Numbers

BEMIDBAR legend

The Rebbe loved HaKotel, (The Wall) — loved the fact that since the destruction of their Temple, his people had chosen a very old retaining wall to be its most sacred place.[1] One Friday, before sunset, he went to the Wall with a disciple to greet Shabbat. As they came down from the Jewish Quarter of the Old City, past Mount Zion and first glimpsed the Wall, the disciple said to the Rebbe, "HaKotel is like our people. Despite everything, we've both survived."

The Rebbe pointed to the Wall and said:

> Do you see those bushes that grow out from the cracks between the stones that make up the Wall? There is barely any soil, yet the bushes grow. The Wall is like the Holy One and we Jews are like those plants. When the Mashiach arrives, those plants will each bloom, sending out a sweet smell that will settle over the earth.

His disciple asked, "What must we do till that time?" The Rebbe answered, "We can only do the best we can do." The student continued, "Then what we do may not be very important." And the Rebbe answered:

> The future of our world may depend on us remembering our own insignificance.

---

[1] This wall supported the plaza on which the Temple sat in ancient Jerusalem.

BEMIDBAR

Numbers 1:1–4:20.

The Levites ... are to camp around the Dwelling [the Tabernacle] and when the Dwelling is to move on, the Levites are to take it down and when the Dwelling is to encamp, the Levites are to set it up....[2]

Levites[3] sometimes brag that they were positioned closest to the Tabernacle, to the Holy Ark, to the Shechinah, because of special virtue they exhibited by siding with Moshe[4] at the time of the Golden Calf.[5]

But there was also a darker side to the Levites. Father Jacob cursed Levi for his wanton killing at Shechem,[6] and said his children, the Levites, would be scattered in the Promised Land.[7]

These two views can be reconciled. A mother may wish to keep her most unruly child closest to her. So too, the Shechinah wanted the Levites to be close in order to watch over them and to guide them with her Loving Presence.[8]

---

[2]Numbers 1:50, 51.

[3]Descendants of Levi, son of Jacob.

[4]The Hebrew name for Moses, used in the Torah.

[5]Exodus 32:26.

[6]Levi, along with his brother Simeon, killed all the males in the town of Shechem in retaliation for the rape of their sister Dina, by the son of the town's ruler. Genesis 34:25.

[7]Genesis 49:5–7.

[8]This strategy was not completely successful since it was Korach, a Levite, who led the Great Rebellion against Moshe. See Numbers, Chapter 16.

NASO legend

*L*ate one afternoon, as the Rebbe walked the streets of B'nai Brak, an orthodox neighborhood on the outskirts of Tel Aviv, a man approached him and asked to talk. They went to a nearby *bet knesset*[9] and sat down. The man began:

"Rebbe, I am a sofer,[10] like my father, like his father, and like his father's father before him. I have been a scribe for many years, beginning by copying the small scrolls inside mezzuzzot and writing marriage contracts. When my work was deemed careful enough and I was deemed devout, I was allowed the sacred privilege of copying Torah scrolls. I am now copying my sixth Torah.

"Like all *soferim* I pray each day before I work, to prepare myself to write every word, every letter, every embellishment of every letter with love for the Holy One and love for the Holy Torah. I have been taught to copy carefully so that my Torah will be like every Torah before it.[11] Today, I completed Chapter 7 of Bemidbar, all 89 verses — more verses than in any other chapter of the Torah. Of course, I copied it word by word, letter by letter — exactly.

"But today I asked myself, why is this chapter so long? The chapter names a prince of each tribe and after naming each prince and his father, spends five verses describing the gifts brought by that prince to consecrate the tabernacle. Each prince brought exactly the same gift. Rebbe, why didn't the Torah simply name each prince and his tribe, list the gifts once and say, "and each and every tribe through its prince brought the same beautiful gifts?"

"If the Holy One had written the Torah that way, then the chapter would have had 55 fewer verses for me to copy and I could have gone home hours earlier today. I know a scribe is not supposed to question the Torah, but Rebbe, do you have an answer?"

---

[9]Literally "house of assembly" but in Israel it is the name most frequently used for "synagogue."

[10]A scribe; plural soferim.

[11]Scribes copy from Tikkun Soferim, books which shows how every word, indeed every letter, of the Torah should appear on a torah scroll.

The Rebbe said:

> Scribe, you show wisdom by questioning. You can approach the Holy One through Torah only if you ask what Torah means.
>
> Go home now. Play with your children. Tomorrow, don't work. Maybe take them to the beach. Every Torah has existed since before the beginning of time. Your work can wait one more day.

ות׳ ות׳ ות׳ ות׳ ות׳ ות׳

NASO

Numbers 4:21–7:89

They shall present their offerings, each prince on his day, for the dedication of the altar.[12]
After the Mishkan had been assembled and the priests had sacrificed the offerings brought by the princes on behalf of each tribe, Moshe could enter the Tent of Meetings and hear the Voice, the Voice of the Holy One coming from above the ark.[13]

Although Moshe alone heard the Voice, he was able to do so only because of the contributions of the entire community. Moshe, therefore, felt obligated to teach Torah to all Israel and to teach all Israel to teach Torah to their children and their children's children.

---

[12]Numbers 7:11.
[13]Numbers 7:89.

BAHA'ALOTECHA legend

And if a stranger shall sojourn with you....[14]

At a dinner in Jerusalem, the Rebbe sat next to an orthodox rabbi from the United States who kept saying that many who considered themselves converts had not been converted according to Halachah[15] and thus were not Jews at all. The Rebbe responded:

> Tomorrow morning, walk down Ben Yehuda Street. You will see red-haired Chasids, and blond Jews from Germany. There will be Jews who look like Yemenites and black Jews who resemble Ethiopians. Do you think that Jacob, Rachel, Leah, Zilpah and Bilhah[16] alone had all those genes? Do you think Jews begin to look like their neighbors merely from living close to them? No. We Jews have always intermarried and I can't believe that every conversion was according to your understanding of Halachah. The Book of Ruth does not mention a conversion of Ruth, the grandmother of King David, from whose house the Messiah will come. Father Abraham himself became a convert.
>
> There are a constant number of Jewish souls in the universe. So many Jews were killed during the Holocaust, that more Jewish souls than Jewish bodies were left. Every convert comes from the Eternal One infusing a Jewish soul into a living being. Are there so many Jews that a few extra are a problem?

---

[14] Numbers 9:14.

[15] The law as interpreted by rabbinic sources.

[16] Jacob and the four mothers of the children of Israel. See Genesis, chapter 29 and 30.

BAHA'ALOTECHA

Numbers 8:1–12:16

They marched from the mountain of Yud Hey Vov Hey, a journey of three days[17].... *And the people complained bitterly....*[18]

As soon as the Israelites left the holy mountain, they began to grumble. At the mountain, they had become so used to the Presence that they felt abandoned when the Shechinah lifted up, even though her purpose was to guide them through the desert to a promised land.

ک‍ی ک‍ی ک‍ی

When the people grumbled for meat, Moshe spoke to the Holy One and then told the people: *tomorrow you will eat meat....*[19] The God you met at Mount Sinai will provide quail. Remember, take no more than you need.

The next day when the quail appeared, not all the Israelites could restrain themselves, some killing more quail than they could possibly eat. This is why Torah tells, *While the meat was still between their teeth, before it was chewed, the anger of Yud Hey Vov Hey blazed forth against the people....*[20]

After that day, the Holy One knew that when the tribes reached their promised homeland, they must never again be given manna.[21]

---

[17]Numbers 10:33.
[18]Numbers 11:1.
[19]Numbers 11:18.
[20]Numbers 11:33.
[21]Joshua 5:12.

SHELACH LECHA legend

One Shabbat in Tel Aviv, as the Rebbe sang Adon Olam, the prayer that concludes the morning service, he saw the beach through the window of his small *bet knesset*. He walked home along the beachfront promenade and passed a young man who recognized him and asked, "Rebbe, is it permissible to surf on Shabbat?" The Rebbe asked him how were the waves and the boy answered, "They are three to four feet and the wind just turned offshore. Their form is perfect."

Thinking of his friend, the High Priest of Aitutaki, the Rebbe answered:

> Would the Holy One permit you to surf only on days when you have to work? Come let us enjoy God's ocean."

SHELACH LECHA

Numbers 13:1–15:41

Send men to spy out the land of Canaan....[22] *And these were their names....*[23]

Ten spies begged Moshe not to place their names in the Torah. But their names had been in the Torah since before the beginning of time. It was this exposure, not their size, that made the ten spies feel as exposed as if they were grasshoppers.[24] They did not believe that Yud Hey Vov Hey would disclose their names, yet protect them. They lost faith, forgetting that their deeds would be remembered for millennia.

Only Joshua and Caleb, the remaining two spies, thought otherwise. *Do not be afraid of the people of the land,*[25] they argued:

> You will remain frightened,
> until you fear becoming afraid.

Because of the ten, the Holy One ordered the taking of the Promised Land to be postponed until after the death of the generation that took part in the Exodus. Since the ten spies thought this a punishment rather than a fulfillment of their wishes, they refused to follow this new instruction. Filled with false confidence, they attempted to take the Promised Land and fought their way to utter defeat.[26]

---

[22]Numbers 13:2.

[23]Numbers 13:4.

[24]*We were in our own eyes like grasshoppers.* Numbers 13:33.

[25]Numbers 14:9.

[26]Numbers 14:45.

KORACH legend

*T*he Rebbe and a disciple visited an old man near death. The old one said he had done things of which he was not proud and asked the Rebbe whether hell might be waiting for him after death. The Rebbe answered:

> Torah does not speak of a hell, only of *Sheol*, a pit. There
> may be a purpose for people to believe there is a hell. But
> what need would the Holy One have to create such a place?

The old man fell asleep and the Rebbe and his student left the room. The disciple asked the Rebbe whether all that he had told the old man was true. The Rebbe sighed and answered:

> How can we know the needs of the Holy One? I have spent
> much of my life wondering about death and whether there
> is an afterlife. Not one second of that time was productive.

KORACH

Numbers 16:1–18:32

When Korach first challenged Moshe for leadership, Moshe was not certain that he even wanted to remain the Israelite's leader, so he said to Korach, *At daybreak Yud Hey Vov Hey will make known who is his and who is holy....*[27]

That night, Moshe went to the Tent of Meetings and said to the Holy One, "Perhaps Korach should become your prophet. The people continue to stray under my leadership."

And the Holy One answered, "Do you think that when my anger rises against Israel, Korach could answer it?"[28] And Moshe knew he must continue, which is why to this day he is known as Moshe Rabbeinu — Moshe our teacher.

In the morning, the Holy One descended to Korach and his followers and at day break, Korach and his servants *went down alive, into the pit [Sheol], the earth closed on them and they perished....*[29]

---

[27]Numbers 16:5.
[28]As Moshe had done, for example, at the time of the Golden Calf. See Exodus 33:11–13.
[29]Numbers 16:33.

CHUKKAT legend

"**W**hat can I learn by studying the rite of the red cow,"[30] asked the Rebbe's student. The Rebbe answered by telling the following parable:

> At the end of a corridor, in the basement of a *yeshiva*, the ceiling light flickered, as it had for months — continually, but to differing rhythms.
>
> The pious students never wished to complain about so trivial a matter. The caretaker never thought it a problem because the flickering bulb gave enough light to allow him to work. The teachers of the *yeshiva* seldom went to the basement and when they did, they were too engrossed in thought to notice this flickering. The *Rosh Yeshiva*, (the spiritual leader) never went to the basement, never heard any complaints about the light.
>
> The learned Rosh understood Hebrew, Aramaic, Arabic, English and Morse code.

The Rebbe continued, "Choose any verse. Study it thoroughly. The more trivial a verse seems, the deeper may be its level of meaning."

---

[30]See Numbers, chapter 19. The ashes of a red cow were used to help purify someone who had become "unclean." The ritual is so obscure that even the ancient Sages despaired of finding its meaning.
[31]Numbers 20:8.

CHUKKAT

Numbers 19:1–22:1

At Meribah, when the Children of Israel had no water, Yud Hey Vov Hey told Moshe to take his rod, the rod that had produced miracles in Egypt, and in front of the Children to speak *to the boulder before their eyes so that it brings forth its water.*[31]

Yud Hey Vov Hey said to Moshe,
Speak to the rock,
   Moshe struck the rock.

I did not say to strike the rock,
I said speak to the rock.
   Is it a great thing?
   At Massah,
   at Horeb,
   you told me to strike the rock
   to bring forth water.[32]

You must listen closely.
   I became impatient, confused.
   Miriam has died.
   I have not yet mourned.

You are Moshe.
I expect more.
   You are El Shaddai.
   I expect more.

You did not believe in me.
   I sanctify you.

But you,
even you,
did not sanctify me in the eyes of the Children.
You cannot lead them
to the Promised Land.[33]
   Moshe sighed
   and knew what was not to be.
   And mourned for sister Miriam
   who saved him by the river Nile.

---

[32]Exodus 17:6.
[33]See Numbers 20:12.

BALAK legend

*T*hen Yud Hey Vov Hey opened the mouth of the ass and she said to Balaam....[34]

The Rebbe was studying parashah Balak with several younger students. Like generations of students before them, they questioned how a donkey could speak. Some of the students argued that it was a miracle, just as the Bible describes other miracles. Some said the Holy One was trying to prevent Balaam, a prophet, from turning towards sin. Still other students said that the story could not literally be true.

When the students finally asked the Rebbe which students were right, the Rebbe answered, You all are." The Rebbe then continued

How can an ass speak?
If a wise man can lie,
then an ass can speak truth.

The Rebbe then continued

There are times a verse is in search of a midrash and times
a midrash searches for a verse.

---

[34]Numbers 22:28.

BALAK

Numbers 22:2–25:9

·

Balaam said, *I will send back to you whatever word Yud Hey Vov Hey speaks to me.*[35]

When Balak, king of Moab, saw the strength of the Israelite army, he sought help from a holy man, rather than from a general. Unfortunately, the holy man Balaam, like the Israelites, believed in Yud Hey Vov Hey.

Some say that Balaam was a greater prophet than Moshe because he believed in Yud Hey Vov Hey and spoke the Holy One's words even though he had not been at Sinai. After going to Mount Pisgah,[36] he saw the future, while later, in the same spot, Moshe saw a land of promise.[37]

But, our Sages tell us that seeing promise takes a greater prophet than seeing the future as if it were the past. But we also honor Balaam by beginning every synagogue service with his words: *How goodly are your tents O Jacob, your dwellings O Israel.*[38]

---

[35]Numbers 22:8.

[36]Numbers 23:14.

[37]Deuteronomy 34:1.

[38]Numbers 24:5. Numbers 31:16 and some rabbinic commentary treat Balaam less favorably.

PINCHAS

*T*he midrash says:
  The vov will remain incomplete until the Mashiach arrives.
His first act will be to fill in the vov in one Torah scroll in Jerusalem. When the dead rise up, the awakened scribes will complete the "shalom" in every other scroll.

The midrash says:

In the days of the Temple, the pious scribe Shmuel died while in the process of writing the word "shalom" in the twelfth verse of the twenty-fifth chapter of Bemidbar. With his last breath, he completed the word shalom. Because of his pain, his hand was not steady and the *vov* was incomplete. When his apprentice completed the scroll, out of respect for Shmuel, he did not complete the *vov*, thinking that surely this must have been the work of the Holy One. To this day, out of respect for the Holy One, out of respect for Shmuel, and most of all out of respect for his loyal apprentice, no scribe completes the *vov*.

۞ ۞ ۞

The Last Rebbe of Bialystok says:

When someone tells you, "The midrash says...." always ask, "Which one?"

---

[39]Numbers 25:12–13.

[40]"The midrash says..." is a formula used by traditionalists to introduce a midrash of ancient origin.

PINCHAS

Numbers 25:10–30:1

give him [Pinchas] *my covenant of shalom* [peace]; *it shall be for him and his descendants after him a covenant of everlasting priesthood....*[39]

שָׁלִים

In parashah *Pinchas*, in the book of Bemidbar, in chapter 25, verse 12, is the word "shalom." In copying Sefrei Torah, scribes are taught that every letter must be copied correctly, every letter in the Torah *except* one: the letter *vov* in the word shalom must be broken in two. Why is space left between the top half of the letter and the bottom?

The midrash says:

Pinchas did as the Holy One wished when he killed both the Israelite man and the sacred prostitute. As a reward, Pinchas and his descendants became High Priests. But a warrior cannot ever know complete peace, so the "shalom" is not completed, the vov is broken.

The midrash says:

Because of the sins of the Israelite men with the daughters of Moab, Yud Hey Vov Hey brought a plague that killed 24,000 Israelites. The vov in "shalom" could not be complete because even the Holy One grieved while thinking of the death of so many of his children.

The midrash says:

It was not necessary for the vov to remain incomplete; Pinchas had only to drop his sword and pick up a pen to complete it.

MATTOT legend

If a man vows a vow to God, or swears an oath to bind himself, he is not to break his word. According to all that goes out of his mouth he is to do.[42]
A man visited the Rebbe and said:

> I feel terrible guilt. When my daughter was ill, and I did not know whether she would live or die, I promised myself that if she recovered, I would wear *t'fillin*[43] and say morning prayers every day for a year. My daughter recovered and I went to morning services for a month, but now many days go by when I am too busy or I just let it pass.

The Rebbe asked, "To whom did you make this vow?" And the man replied, "I said it to myself." The Rebbe continued, "Did you say it aloud or silently?" And the man answered that he had been silent.

The Rebbe then said:

> You need not feel shame. You did not make a vow. Torah carefully tells us that a thought is not a vow unless it proceeds out of the mouth, crosses the lips. Not even the Almighty can keep track of people's random thoughts. Certainly, no man or woman can.
>
> Don't forget, however, even though you've made no vow, you may wish to thank the Holy One for the good health of your daughter.

---

[42]Numbers 30:3. Deuteronomy 23:22–24 makes clear that it is better to avoid making a vow than to risk breaking one.

[43]*T'fillin* are small boxes containing Hebrew prayers which traditional Jewish men wear during weekday morning prayers. The boxes are attached to leather straps which allow them to be worn, one on the forehead and the other on the left arm. See Exodus 13:9.

MATTOT

Numbers 30:2–32:42

*Y*ud Hey Vov Hey *spoke to Moshe saying: Seek vengeance, the vengeance of the Children of Israel from the Midianites.*[44]

As a younger man, Moshe had hoped that it would not be necessary for God to kill all the first born Egyptians.[45] Torah records, however, that when he was older, he did not object to Yud Hey Vov Hey's plan to kill the Midianites. In fact, Moshe was furious with his military commanders for not having killed all the Midianites' male children.[46] Yet, the Midianites had given Moshe shelter when he first fled from Egypt.[47] And the Midianite woman Tsippora, (Yitro's daughter), was Moshe's wife, the mother of his sons.

When Abraham learned of Yud Hey Vov Hey's plan to kill the people of Sodom, he tried to dissuade the Holy One.[48] When Abraham was told to sacrifice Isaac, he prepared to do so, but listened for the voice which would change that command.[49]

Because of the different reactions of Abraham and Moshe, some say that even though Moshe was the greater prophet, Abraham was more of a *mensch*.[50]

---

[44]Numbers 31:1,2.

[45]See the midrash for parashah Bo.

[46]Numbers 31:14–17.

[47]Exodus 2:15.

[48]Genesis chapter 18.

[49]Genesis chapter 22.

[50]"Mensch" literally means "man" in Yiddish. But the closest American equivalent might be "stand-up guy."

MASSEY legend

The Rebbe preached to give *tzedaka*[51] to all those in need. The Rebbe taught that the Mashiach — the messiah — the savior — would first appear in rags, and would be unable to complete the journey until first shown an act of loving kindness.

One day the Rebbe walked the streets of Jerusalem's old city, accompanied by a disciple. As they passed the Jewish Quarter, they saw two old women begging on opposite sides of the street. The disciple told the Rebbe, "I do not have even a shekel with me."

The Rebbe reached into his own pocket and found only one coin. He looked at the two women and gave it to the impoverished, old woman on his right. When they passed, the disciple asked the Rebbe, "What if the other woman were the waiting Mashiach?"

The Rebbe replied, "Then surely I have acted correctly. An impoverished, old woman needs a shekel more than the Mashiach does."

---

[51] The word "tzedaka" can mean righteousness or justice. It often, as here, means an act of charity, certainly one of its aspects.

MASSEY

Numbers 33:1–36:13

*T*hese are the marching stages of the Children of Israel that they went out from the land of Egypt....[52] They set out from the wilderness of Sinai and camped at Kibroth-hattavah.[53]

Torah makes little mention of the events that took place during the middle thirty-eight years of the forty years the Israelites wandered in the wilderness. Yet parashah Massey lists many places where they set up camps during that period.

Some say that because those sites are included in the Torah, their names must be important, but that events from that period that were not included were not important.

Yet others say we can learn much from studying about the missing events during the thirty-eight years. How could it be otherwise, they ask, for in this period the generation of the Exodus died and the generation that would take the Promised Land was born. They believe that the events of these years were not told in order to allow those who study Torah to establish midrashim.

Finally, there are those who think the names of the camping places were included, but other events were excluded to help teach how thin a line separates being from not being.

---

[52]Numbers 33:1.
[53]Numbers 33:16.

דברים

Devarim

Deuteronomy

DEVARIM legend

A student with whom the Rebbe had been studying parashah Devarim noted a difference between the account of the spies in Deuteronomy and the narrative of the same events in Numbers. Numbers suggests that the idea to send spies to view the Promised land originated with God and was conveyed by Moses to the Israelites.[1] Yet Deuteronomy suggests that the Israelites initiated the idea of the mission.[2]

The student said to the Rebbe, "I cannot accept the argument that the problem is solved merely by applying the doctrine that Torah must be read to make no word redundant. The two narratives are too inconsistent."

The Rebbe agreed and said:

> For difficult passages, you and I may have to write the Torah.

---

[1]See Numbers 13:1–3.
[2]Deuteronomy 1:22.

DEVARIM

Deuteronomy 1:1–3:22

T *hese are the words that Moishe spoke to all Israel on the other side of the Jordan....*[3]

How could Moishe, one old man with one stuttering voice speak to *all* Israel? Some doubt this event actually occurred, except in the most literal sense. They say that Moishe spoke to all Israel, but not all Israel was able to hear.

Others believe that all Israel heard. They say that Moishe told the rulers of thousands, who told the rulers of hundreds, who told the rulers of fifty,[4] who told the rest of the Israelites. Those who believe this conclude that with the retellings, each group of Israelites heard a slightly different Torah.

There is one further explanation. Since every Jew who ever lived, or whoever will live was at Sinai, all Israel already knew Torah and thus could understand Moishe whether or not they heard his voice.

---

[3]Deuteronomy 1:1.
[4]See Deuteronomy 1:15, which establishes this administrative structure.

VA'ETCHANAN legend

*O*ne evening, the Rebbe studied parashah Va'etchanan with an old man who had survived the death camps. On reading, *We were Pharaoh's slaves in Egypt, and the Lord brought us out of Egypt with a mighty hand,*[5] the man asked the Rebbe:

> If God could save Israel from Egypt, why didn't God intervene at Auschwitz? Even if God usually no longer takes part in the events of history, surely the Holocaust was time for an exception. Only a Jew who is an idiot could still believe there is an all-powerful, benevolent God who controls the destiny of the universe.

The Rebbe agreed and suggested they return to learning the ten commandments as set out in Va'etchanan.

---

[5]Deuteronomy 6:21.

VA'ETCHANAN

Deuteronomy 3:23–7:11.

*N*ow *I pleaded with Yud Hey Vov Hey...let me cross that I may see the good land that is beyond the Jordan.*[6]

Yud Hey Vov Hey said to Moishe, "I told you I would not let you lead the people into the Promised Land. But Moishe, go climb Mount Pisgah so you may at least see it."

As Moishe prepared for the climb,[7] he tried to remember that although he could not enter the Promised Land, his Torah would.

ﻌ ﻌ ﻌ

You are not to add to the word that I am commanding you, and you are not to subtract from it....[8]

The Eternal One wished to forbid the Israelites from diminishing any of the commandments. But Moishe said, "First, first (and this was Moishe repeating for emphasis, not merely stuttering) you must forbid them from adding to the law. Zealots can do more harm than backsliders."[9]

---

[6]Deuteronomy 3:24–26.
[7]See Deuteronomy 34:1 and discussion of Vezot Habrachah.
[8]Deuteronomy 4:2, 13:1.
[9]Here, as in the legend set out in the discussion of Mishpatim, the Rebbe limits the doctrine of building "a fence" around the Torah.

EKEV legend

*Y*ou are to write [these words] *on the doorposts of your house and your gates....*[10]

It is said that the Rebbe once met with the wise elders of Chelm. "The young people of our town," they said, "no longer kiss the *mezzuzot*[11] when they enter and leave their homes. What should we do, Rebbe?"

The Rebbe answered:
> Take down the *mezzuzot*. Then there will be nothing for the young to fail to kiss."

The oldest of the men from Chelm shook his head sadly and answered, "Rebbe, how about you give us a solution and let us make the jokes. Do you take us for a bunch of fools?"[12]

ﻬ ﻬ ﻬ

The Rebbe was frank with the businessman from Chelm, telling him that he saw no chance for profit in manufacturing a combination *mezzuzah*-doorbell.

---

[10]Deuteronomy 11:20.

[11]Jews place a small case called a mezzuzah, (plural mezzuzot) usually of metal, on their doorposts. Inside are passages from the Torah, written by a scribe. It is the custom when entering or leaving a home with a mezzuzah to touch the mezzuzah with one's fingers and then to kiss those fingers.

[12]The "Wise Men of Chelm" are creations of Jewish folklore. Although they are called chachemim (wise men), this is said sarcastically because they act as fools. What has happened here is that someone has created a joke, treating the "Wise Men" as if they were real.

In southern Poland, there is an actual town of Chelm. It is difficult to know whether its Jews were more or less wise than other Jews of Poland since almost all Polish Jews were murdered during the Holocaust.

EKEV

Deuteronomy 7:12–11:25

*I*n Moishe's plea to the people he asked:

> *And now Israel what does the Lord your God ask of you except to hold God in awe, to walk in all God's ways and to love God and to serve God with all your heart and all your soul?*[13]

Moishe had thought instead of saying

> *And what the Lord requires of you is only to do justly, and to love mercy, and to walk humbly with your God.*[14]

But Moishe knew that centuries later a spokesman for the oppressed would arise one day who would need those words to persuade the Kingdom of Judah. Moishe left the words unsaid, so they would be available for the prophet Micah.

---

[13]Deuteronomy 10:12.
[14]Micah 6:8.

RE'EH legend

*O*n Simchat Torah,[15] the Rebbe visited a synagogue in a distant town and noticed sadness in the face of a congregant. The Rebbe approached him and asked if there were anything he could do to help. The man told the Rebbe that he was depressed, that he had given up hope. The man continued that he had tried to raise his spirits for the holiday, but now he felt even worse because he could not feel joy even on the evening of Simchat Torah.

The Rebbe hugged the man and said:

> Didn't the blessed Naomi, say: *Call me Marah* [bitter] *for the Almighty dealt very bitterly with me?*[16]
>
> Torah has to direct, *You are to rejoice on your festivals*[17] because at times it is so difficult a thing to do. The Holy One did not give you Simchat Torah in order to add to your burden.

---

[15]Simchat Torah (Joy of Torah) is celebrated on the last day of the holiday of Succot, the fall harvest festival. On Simchat Torah, the reading of Deuteronomy is completed and the reading of Genesis is begun, to symbolize the seamless nature of Torah study. It is a holiday usually celebrated in great happiness.

[16]Ruth 1:20.

[17]Deuteronomy 16:14.

RE'EH

Deuteronomy 11:26–16:17

*I*t *shall be in the place that Yud Hey Vov Hey, your God, chooses to have his name dwell....*[18]

It is never revealed in the Five Books that Jerusalem would become the resting place of the Holy Name. Surely Yud Hey Vov Hey already knew that the House, the Sanctuary, would be built at the very spot where Abraham bound Isaac.[19] Some say Moishe guessed this, but did not tell the Israelites, fearing that if he told them, the tribes would fight each other to control the territory closest to the Shechinah's home.

Moishe meant well, but if he had been more forthcoming he might have prevented the disintegration of Solomon's Kingdom, centuries later.

---

[18]Deuteronomy 12:11.

[19]By tradition, Isaac's redemption occurred in what is today Jerusalem, on the very rock that is now beneath the Dome of the Rock.

SHOFTIM legend

*T*he Rebbe studied parashah Shoftim with an Israeli who had fought in several of Israel's wars. After some discussion of the parashah, the man said to the Rebbe, "When I read descriptions of the wars which God allowed and encouraged, and when I read of God's anger towards the Israelites, I think that Torah gives an immature view of God. I know what it means to destroy and I know what it means to be destroyed." The Rebbe answered:

Perhaps Torah gives an accurate view of an immature God. I must admit, there are times I feel I am hurtling through the universe with a child, or even a madman, at the helm.

Try to do God's work, even when it is not clear what is required. When in doubt, work for peace. God may need your assistance.[20]

---

[20]A theme in many of the Rebbe's midrashim (see, for example, Bereshit) is that the righteous must take part in the ongoing process of Creation.

SHOFTIM

Deuteronomy 16:18–21:9

arashah Shoftim states:

Justice, Justice shall you pursue...[21]

This concept is so simple, yet so profound, that to understand the verse is to accept it. Once all accept it, the Messiah can arrive, as it is said, In the world-to-come, the only midrash will be the one that explains why midrashim are no longer needed.

જ જ જ

How can the same parashah also say:

You shall utterly destroy them: the Hittite, the Amorite, the Canaanite, the Perizzite, Hivite and the Jebusite.[22]

It couldn't. The verse cannot mean what it appears to mean on the surface.[23] To pursue justice, find a midrash which explains the verse's true meaning.[24] That is why there are metaphors.[25]

---

[21]Deuteronomy 16:20.

[22]Deuteronomy 20:17.

[23]The Jerusalem Talmud as well as Medieval Jewish scholars searched for alternatives to the literal meaning of this verse.

[24]The Rebbe taught that new or unsolved problems create the need for new midrashim.

[25]The Rebbe continues this theme of understanding Torah concepts on a symbolic level in Ki Tetze, next week's parashah.

KI TETZE legend

*W*hen teaching material for which there is no clear answer, such as the reason for the rule prohibiting *shaatness*, the Rebbe would focus on the notion of paradox.

THE PARADOX PARADOX

There is no answer to the question of whether one should try to answer a paradox, since the question itself is a paradox.

THE SUGGESTION BOX PARADOX

A messenger once visited a factory and saw a suggestion box. He wondered where the person who had suggested the box had placed that suggestion? Did the existence of the box, then, negate its necessity?

ॐ ॐ ॐ

How could someone truthfully be the first to say, "There is nothing new under the sun?"[26]

---

[26]Kohelat, (Ecclesiastics) 1:9.

KI TETZE

Deuteronomy 21:10–25:19

You are not to sow your vineyard with two kinds.... [of crops] *You are not to plow with an ox and a donkey together. You are not to clothe yourself in wool and linen together* [shaatnes][27]

It is only symbolically that one can understand why Torah forbids the mingling of two types of crops in a field, the mingling of two types of work animals, the mingling of linen and wool in a garment, but commands the mingling of threads in the four corners of garments.[28]

One cannot understand a symbolism unless one understands the underlying symbols. Thus, those who obey the prohibitions against mingling lose the ability to understand those minglings as symbols. For them, understanding the prohibitions against mixing can only be approached by contemplating the twisting (the mixing) of the threads.

---

[27]Deuteronomy 22:9–11.

[28]*Twisted cords you are to make yourself on the four corners of your covering....* Deuteronomy 22:12. Jewish men traditionally wear prayer shawls with fringes of twisted threads in the corners. Orthodox men also wear undershirts with twisted threads in the corners. These twisted cords are called tzitzis.

KI TAVO legend

student of the Rebbe asked him

> I know that our Sages say that the study of Torah is equal
> to all the other commandments because it leads to them
> all. But I am new to Torah and not a scholar. When I read
> Ki Tavo, with its long list of curses that will befall the
> Israelites if they do not follow God's way,[29] I am unable to
> study. My mind goes blank.

The Rebbe answered

> There are many entrances to the House of the Holy One.
> For you, perhaps it is best to approach it through prayer.

"I don't know how to pray as a Jew."

> Then pray.

"But I don't know how to pray, Rebbe."

> One need not know how to pray in order to pray.
> One learns to pray by praying.

"Will prayer bring me joy?"

> Joy is more likely to bring you to prayer.

---

[29]Deuteronomy 28:15–68.

KI TAVO

Deuteronomy 26:1–29:8

*M*oishe thought it a mistake for HaShem to give the Israelites a new set of "Warnings,"[30] (a list of horrible consequences that would occur from failing to follow the commandments) and to instruct the Israelites to read them from mountain tops once they crossed the Jordan.[31] Moishe said to Yud Hey Vov Hey:

> The warnings you already gave in the Book of Vayyikra[32] were scary enough. Giving a second set of blessings and curses, and having the Israelites recite them from opposing mountains in the Promised Land will impress them more. Too much fear may paralyze the people.

And the Holy One answered:

> The people have a frightening task: conquering Canaan. That fear must be balanced by the fear of failing to carry out my commandments. Give them the warning.

Moishe knew he had to follow HaShem's commandment. But when he recited the instructions to the elders, he stuttered to such a degree it was nearly impossible for them to understand him.

---

[30]Deuteronomy 28:15–68
[31]Deuteronomy 27:11–14.
[32]Leviticus 26:14–39.

NITZAVIM legend

*L*ate at night, a student asked the Rebbe, "If we Jews have an everlasting covenant with God, why have we been made to suffer so much?"

The Rebbe answered:

> Our people have suffered. But it is not we alone among the nations who have suffered. Don't you think the Amorite, the Hivite, and the Jebusite each suffered in their turn? The reason we remember our suffering is because we survived and we continue to read our history.

The student said, "But surely this is not an answer to why the Holocaust occurred." The Rebbe paused in deep thought and answered:

> No, it isn't. I need to think. Perhaps the Covenant the Holy One made with our ancestors has been shattered and the task is now for Jews to forge a new covenant, with better terms than the last. We cannot make believe that what happened did not happen.

NITZAVIM

Deuteronomy 29:9–30:20

The hidden things are for Yud Hey Vov Hey our God, but the revealed things are for us and our children for ever to observe all the words of this law.[33]

In each and every Torah scroll, scribes place dots over each letter in the Hebrew words that mean "for us and our children." There are many explanations for those dots,[34] but in truth, it is just one more hidden thing that is not revealed.

৯ ৯ ৯

The Holy One made covenants with Abraham, Isaac and Jacob, which bound their descendants. And every Jew whoever lived, or whoever will live, took part in the Covenant at Sinai. Why then did Moshe insist that the people covenant again as they entered the Promised Land?[35]

It was to give each Israelite one more opportunity to *Choose Life.*[36] A covenant in perpetuity with the Holy One must be renewed day after day after day, just as we must choose life day after day after day.

---

[33]Deuteronomy 29:28.

[34]There are fifteen verses in Torah which have such dotted words. Various explanations have been given for them. Some explain that these dots call attention to particularly important concepts. Others claim that ancient scribes dotted words when they made slight alterations from source texts which they feared had incorporated earlier errors.

[35]Deuteronomy 29:11.

[36]Deuteronomy 30:19.

VAYYELACH legend

*I*n a remote desert town visited by the Rebbe, a downcast middle aged man approached him and cried, "My life is half over. I have never read Torah. I am poor. My body aches. My spirit is depressed."

The Rebbe smiled at the man and said:

Study Torah.

The Rebbe returned to the town five years later and saw the same man, still looking downcast. The man approached the Rebbe again and asked, "Remember me? I have studied Torah for five years. My body aches more now than before and I am still poor, still depressed."

The Rebbe smiled and answered:

I can see that what you say is true. But you have learned Torah.

VAYYELACH

Deuteronomy 31:1–30

*N*ow *Moses spoke these words to all Israel. He said to them — a hundred and twenty years old am I today. I am no longer able to go out and come in....*[37]

Now Moses was a hundred and twenty years old at his death; his eyes had not grown dim, his vigor had not fled.[38]

Torah says Moses' vigor had not fled, that his eyes had not gone dim. But Moses said that he was no longer able to go out and come in. How can this be?

When Moses said that he was unable to go out and come in, he was referring to the fact that the Holy One had forbidden him from going out of the desert and from coming into the Holy Land.

When Torah says that Moses' eyes had not gone dim, it means that he was still a prophet, able to look into the future and see it.[39]

---

[37] Deuteronomy 31:1–2.

[38] Deuteronomy 34:7.

[39] Some rabbinic interpretations treat Deuteronomy 32:14–23 as if the verses are prophecy of harms that will befall the Israelites in the future, at the hands of the Babylonians and the Romans.

HAAZINU legend[40]

*I*n the forest,
beneath the tree
    — the old tree —
leaves blot out the sun.
Souls are silent,
perhaps at peace,
more likely simply gone.
    A frog croaks,
     another answers back.

In the town,
beneath the house,
    — the old house —
Two children hide
from soldiers sent to kill.
    One child screams,
     the other dares not answer back.

In my heart
beneath my soul,
a silent scream answers the child.
    Rain slips
     through the leaves.

---

[40]The above poem, dealing with the Holocaust, or an earlier pogrom was
given to me by the man I met in Jerusalem that I discuss in the epilogue.

HAAZINU

Deuteronomy 32:1–52

All Torah came from HaShem except the Song of Moishe[41] which was composed by Moishe alone. When he had just a few days left on earth, he said to the Eternal One:

> The Israelites will remember
>> a warrior
>> and a teacher,
>> a scribe,
>> and a prophet.
>
> Let them also remember
>> a poet
>> and a singer of songs.
>
> I sang to you, my Holy One,
>> when I reached the desert.
>
> May I sing to you again
>> as I leave?

So HaShem said, "Moishe, my friend, now write yourself down your Song...." And that is why the Song of Moishe begins with Moishe saying:

> *Give ear O heaven and I will speak;*
> *and let the earth hear the words of my mouth.*[42]

---

[41]Deuteronomy 32:1–43. Some also credit Moses with The Song at the Red Sea (Exodus 15:1–18) and Psalm 90.

[42]Deuteronomy 32:1.

VEZOT HABRACHAH legend

*P*reparing for that evening's celebration of Simchat Torah, the Rebbe met with several of his students who were completing their study of the entire cycle of the Five Books for the first time. The Rebbe wished them mazel tov, and then cautioned them against failing to read the Torah again. He said:

> If one's perception of Torah becomes fixed, one can no longer confront the Holy One through study. But when you read the Torah again, you can view it with new eyes because you already know the text's ending. It is for this reason that on Simchat Torah, when we finish parashah Vezot Habrachah and begin Bereshit, we celebrate not the death of Moishe Rabbeinu, but the life of Moishe our teacher.

A student asked the Rebbe whether the Exodus story isn't a greater celebration of the life of Moishe. The Rebbe answered:

> The sun is setting. Enough talk.
>> Let's sing and dance and eat and drink some schnapps and give thanks for the gift of Torah.

VEZOT HABRACHAH

Deuteronomy 33:1–34:12

*N*ow *Moishe went up from the plains of Moab to Mount Nebo....*[44]

Moishe, servant of Yud Hey Vov Hey, died there in the land of Moab, at the order of Yud Hey Vov Hey.[45]

As Moishe climbed Mount Nebo, he asked HaShem
What will death be like?
  And HaShem answered:
  Look at the land I show you.
The land where I cannot set my feet.
  Look to your past.
A land to which I cannot return.
Blessed One, I am frightened.
  You were frightened when you climbed Mount Sinai,
  frightened to receive the Law.
But where am I to go?
  To your end.
  Where you started.
  It's quite simple.
  Nothing more to do.
  Bereshit.

---

[44]Deuteronomy 34:1.
[45]Deuteronomy 34:5–6.

EPILOGUE

As I neared completion of this project, one Saturday morning, I attended services at the Bialystok Synagogue on New York's Lower East Side. The block of Willett Street on which it stands just south of Delancey is now called Bialystoker Place. The building began life as a church, but was converted to a synagogue when the Lower East Side became the center of Jewish life in America. I approached the Synagogue walking past Chinese children who were replacing Puerto Rican children who had replaced the Jewish children who had replaced Irish children and so on, ever since Dutch children replaced Indian children in a process that most likely went back even further than that.

The synagogue recently had been elaborately restored; the beautiful zodiac design ceiling was once again vibrant. At the end of services, I talked with one of the older men in the congregation and asked him if any Bialystokers were members. He told me no, and suggested that I try visiting the nearby Bialystoker Nursing Home.

The following Monday morning I returned to the Lower East Side to visit the nursing home. At the reception desk, I asked to see an administrator. When she greeted me, I asked if any Bialystokers lived in the Home. She told me just one and brought me to him.

He had been born in Bialystok in 1911 and immigrated to the United States twelve years later. When I told him of my interest in Bialystok, he seemed very happy to see me, which he showed by crying. He said:

> I'm the only Bialystoker here. Everyone is a stranger. They're all strangers. No other Bialystokers. No pictures of the old fish market. Only pictures of cats and dogs.

I asked if he ever heard of a Last Rebbe of Bialystok.

I knew many rabbis.

But do you know of a last one?

Everyone here is a stranger.

Tell me about the rabbis you did know.

Do you play three-handed pinochle?

My father taught me when I was young, but I've forgotten how.

It doesn't matter. We'd never find a third.

I told myself that I would return to visit him again. About two weeks later I returned, looked in on him, saw he was asleep, and left.

I then felt a need to visit both Poland and Israel in a last attempt to learn more about the Last Rebbe of Bialystok.

Arriving in Bialystok, I learned only what I already knew — one must search to find evidence that not very long ago, this was a Jewish city: a Hebrew plaque here, a memorial there, but almost never a breathing, living Jew. The city's memorial to its heroes and martyrs does not mention that 80% of them were Jewish. Polish children play soccer on their field, mercifully unaware that the bones of murdered Jewish children lie beneath their running feet. As I looked at the city's Stalinesque apartment blocks, and even its older sections with ancient wooden homes and unpaved streets, I realized how completely separate the present geographic reality has become from the past I imagine.

Yet from 1830–1941, when controlled by Russia and when controlled by Poland, Bialystok was probably the largest city in the world with a Jewish majority. This was not a small shtetl town, but a major city — a place of both religious and secular learning. Today, I could find no one there who had heard of any Rebbe of Bialystok and very few who seemed aware of the city's Jewish past. I heard legends that reminded me of some attributed to the Rebbe, but in Bialystok today they were always attributed to a Catholic priest whose existence I also could not confirm.

I left Bialystok, driving towards Warsaw. Though I had not planned it, I took a by-road to Treblinka, now a memorial park. I drove through a peaceful landscape. Near the entrance, I crossed a bridge under which a peasant farmer fished. I toured the death camp, knowing only that it was good to be allowed to leave. I wished I could understand my visit, put words to the feelings, but realized that those words, for me, must come from my children and their children.

I flew from Warsaw directly to Israel. On my first morning in Jerusalem, I sat in a cafe and talked with an old man with whom I shared a table. He spoke English with a Yiddish, rather than an Israeli, accent. I told him that while in Poland I had visited Treblinka.

The old man told me that only recently he too had returned from a trip to Poland, the land where he had been born. He continued:

> I visited Warsaw, saw no Jews and realized my Warsaw no longer exists. I returned to Bialystok, met no Jews and realized even my Bialystok no longer exists. I went to the forests behind Bialystok and heard only the silence of Jewish partisans, dead souls who refuse to say Kaddish[1] for the living.

I asked him how I could believe in God after visiting Treblinka. He answered:

> I understand. I don't know how it is possible. The Holy One was not in that place, only the messenger of death.

The man then motioned his arms, taking in all of Jerusalem and continued:

---

[1] A prayer used for many purposes, including praying for the dead.

HaShem may not even be in this place. You and I both must help the Shechinah to return. It may be easier for you to give up Poland than to give up the Holy One. Poland was not your time, not your place. Let it go. Return to your family. Create. Poland was not Jerusalem.

As I got ready to leave, I said to him, "I mean no offense, but I wish to ask you something." And he responded, "Yes"

"Are you.....
Yes?
"Were you....
Yes?
"Ah....
I cannot tell you who I am, or who I was, until you tell me whom you want me to be.

I wished him peace, took my leave, and returned to the States.